Net Making

To my wife
for her encouragement
and for her patience with the 'everlasting string'

Net Making

Charles Holdgate, B.A.

*with drawings by the author
and photographs by Alec Davis*

EMERSON BOOKS, INC.
Buchanan, New York

Contents

Introduction

Recently I asked a class of the oldest boys in the school to empty their pockets. Every boy had a handkerchief, some had small amounts of money and the appropriate ones had the price of the school meal, but there was woefully little else in any pocket. Forty years ago, not every boy would have had a handkerchief, few any money, but each would have had his collection of treasures—an army cap badge, a piece of lead, a cheap pocket compass (cased in tin with a mirror at the back), the odd marble in season and inevitably a piece of string.

What a sad degenerate state—stringless boys! We cannot simply blame Scotch tape. Fortunately the situation is easily rectified. There must be something basic about string for I find that children, especially boys, have only to be introduced to string and they are happy.

To help return to this blessed state of children happily and creatively 'playing with string', I offer this book of netting with a justified confidence that they are of proven appeal to children, especially, but not only, to boys.

All the patterns have been worked successfully with children of 9, 10 and 11 years old and if followed will produce a quick and satisfying result. BUT IN ALL MODESTY AND HUMILITY, MAY I ASK ALL WHO ARE KIND ENOUGH TO USE THEM TO FOLLOW THE PATTERNS IN THE FIRST PLACE EXACTLY AS PRINTED. After that, vary the patterns as you wish, particularly by enlarging, for as far as is consistent with practical usefulness the patterns have been designed as economically as possible—that is with a large size mesh and a minimum number of meshes—in order to achieve a quick and effective result. All can be expanded, the bottle carrier to a full-sized bag and the shopping bag to a family-size bag which will take all the king-size, giant and magnum packets of cereals, detergents, etc., together with all their free offers.

Although planned originally for teachers and their children in schools, the material comprising this book has been found to be of great interest and considerable assistance to a great many people who are not concerned with teaching, merely with learning and practicing the craft for themselves as a hobby, for profit or merely as something they had always wanted to do. I am delighted to cite my oldest enthusiast, Charles F. Swaine, aged 70, retired, with the time and the desire to learn and to do; he learned readily and has found a new and satisfying craft.

Judging by the number of inquiries, by teachers and non-teachers alike, I am confident that many adults will find this book of great private interest and help, that any adult can work through the course to teach himself, whether or not he may wish to pass on the craft to others. So I offer this book believing that it will be of help to individual people and to groups like the women's organizations, to occupational therapists and their patients, to Scouts, Sea Scouts, youth clubs, 4-H clubs, to senior citizens, and probably most of all to people in need of a simple fireside hobby.

Chapter 1
What you will need

String

This need not be elaborate to start with. Have plenty of white cotton twine, medium thick (referred to as #20 shearer cord) and a few half-pound balls of the same twine, thick (referred to as #60 shearer cord).

As an alternative, macrame twine is readily available in most craft shops. It is sold natural and colored, in cotton, jute, hemp, linen, flax, as well as in nylon and other synthetics, (braided, corded, flat, waxed and unwaxed).

Netting needles

These are the string holders, usually made of flexible and almost unbreakable plastic. They are obtainable from suppliers of craft materials and some anglers' shops.

If you have difficulty obtaining netting needles, write to the manufacturer:
Linen Thread Company, Blue Mountain, Alabama 36201.
They will send you the name of their closest retail outlet.

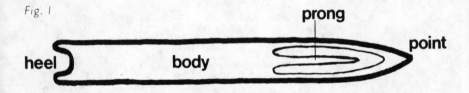

Fig. 1

prong

point

heel   body

If you are thinking of setting up a netting group you should start with enough medium sized needles (approximately $\frac{3}{4}$ inch wide) for one each and a few spares, enough small needles ($\frac{1}{2}$ inch wide) for two each and spares, and a few large needles (about $\frac{7}{8}$ inch wide) for occasional use.

Mesh sticks

The mesh stick performs two functions; it determines the size of the mesh and ensures that the meshes are all equal in size. Care should be taken to use the sizes of mesh stick and needle specified in the patterns for the mesh stick must always be rather wider than the needle so that the loaded needle will pass comfortably through the meshes.

They are made in thin, smooth wood, especially beech, but can be improvised from thick or medium strawboard, old rulers, etc. They should be rectangular in shape, about 6 to 8 inches long and in widths required for the various mesh sizes. For these patterns, mesh sticks in 1 inch, $1\frac{1}{2}$ and 2 inch widths will be needed for each person.

Colored plexiglass is not too difficult to cut and smooth and the attractiveness of mesh sticks in this material makes the labor worth while.

Hooks

Cup hooks attached at suitable heights in safe and convenient places. Coat pegs in the cloakroom will suffice; a portable coat-rack or any wooden frame will make a good netting rack for a reasonable sized group. The author uses old swing blackboard frames with the board removed and the top bar lowered. One frame accommodates eight children, either standing to work with their netting attached to the top bar, or seated with their netting attached to the lower bar.

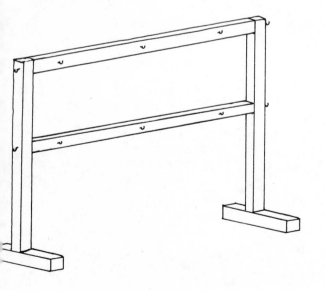

Fig. 2

It is well to remember that netting can be done more efficiently if it is attached to a hook slightly higher than the netter's chest so that the work slopes up and away from him.

S-*shaped hooks*

Butcher's hooks with the points hack-sawed or filed off, metal rod or strong wire bent to a similar shape and size are useful for hanging work between two chair backs when making string handles on shopping bags.

Buttons

These are threaded with a string loop to make a toggle with which to suspend circular netting for bags so that it rotates freely. Trouser and jacket buttons are a good size, but do have a good stock, for enthusiastic netters will cut off their own buttons to supply an urgent need!

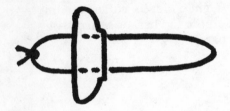

Fig. 3

Chapter 2

Netting as a group activity

This Chapter has been specially written for teachers:
Non-teachers should carry on with Chapter 3.

The question most teachers want answered is how they can begin netting as a class or group activity. You can work up to a large group of 24 or more on netting by starting successive groups of four at a time. To the complete novice in netting I would recommend the following approach:

First of all, become reasonably proficient yourself. You do not need to be such an expert as to be able to push aside a tough trawlermen and take over his mending of a badly torn trawl net. But you must be sufficiently familiar with the patterns to be able to recognize mistakes, diagnose them, remedy them and take steps to prevent their recurrence. To help you do this, I suggest in all modesty that this book is designed specifically for that purpose. It is based entirely on work planned for and used (a) with children of 9, 10 and 11 years and (b) in courses for teachers. I have tried to be detailed and explicit, knowing how complicated netting can appear. Those who take to it readily will skip what are to them unnecessary repetitions, while those who have to plod will I hope find the steps so closely detailed that no step is too big to be taken comfortably. I have also tried not to write a book on netting which is too general but one which can be used by busy teachers and is so programmed that it can be followed from beginning to end for a complete and sequential course for teachers and children, with enough repetition for reinforcement and a steady rate for introducing new processes. At the same time I have added extra material as a reference section to which the teacher once proficient may wish to refer, either to develop the course for older and abler children or possibly merely for his own interest and benefit.

Secondly, having mastered enough of the craft yourself, teach it to four children with good coordination. (The remainder of the class will continue on established activities or, if this is a first venture into group crafts, on an activity which is easily set up and can be managed with relatively little attention, e.g. painting.) Once these four children are established, that is once they can manage the shaped single-color shopping bag with its increases, they are the experts and tell them so; they can be expected to help the next four. Initiate four more children and set them to work under the first group's supervision; the first group do no netting of their own until the second group are independent. Once the second group are established, set the first group on the next stage of the course and initiate four more new ones to work under the supervision of the second set of experts. This develops successfully and when the teacher has his hands full and someone needs urgent help, a cry of 'Who can help so-and-so with such-and-such?' will find immediate help forthcoming. In addition, some children are willing to watch others being taught before they themselves can be included in the group, and provided they are not a nuisance and are not too numerous, this can be encouraged. Besides, those who watch lose nothing by it, they can even be of help with extra fingers to help sort difficult loops and in any case help you decide who are the next keenest four to be initiated.

Obviously to work with any numbers at all there has to be organization. Children must be able to find their own work, needles, mesh sticks and to put them back again tidily. Plastic bags with name cards visible from outside or paper bags with names written on the outside help to keep work separate, untangled and easily found at the beginning of the lesson. They must be able to help themselves to the required amounts of string without waste or tangling the supply; always insist that string is served from the middle of the ball or is pre-wound on a suitable dispenser. I found that a line drier designed for fishing lines did good service. By making a few additional turns, fresh supplies of string can easily be laid on. A very simple winder and dispenser for string can be made with a base-board and a 6-inch nail. Above all, have a set place for scissors; a limited number at strategic points are better than too many, but have a strict rule that scissors are returned to their place after use. A waste basket or box is necessary for real waste and a place for odd remnants of string which may be useful; a regular habit of hanging these pieces evenly by a hook makes them easy to collect later and hang in a loop for easy withdrawal when required. Anyone can then select one end of a suitable length of string and withdraw it without tangling the rest. In any case you may as well be prepared; you can expect to be besieged with requests for odd pieces of string both from children to take home to practise knots and plaits and from colleagues. The simple answer to this is that if there is any string in the odd remnants loop, very well, but if not and it means cutting from a ball, then you very much regret there is none available. Another useful time-saver and preserver of sanity is to have this book available for children to use or reduce the patterns to a suitable shorthand and inscribe them on the mesh sticks, e.g. the football or basketball carrier—11 + 1 for 5 rows. This would mean cast on 11 loops, make a grommet, tie off and make the extra loop; then mesh for 5 rows.

I am well aware how irritating it can be to the beginner to be
told he will think of many other items for himself and I have tried
earnestly to give full information about all the needs I found.
However I know that one person's difficulties are not necessarily
another's, but am confident that teachers will not be content to
muddle through and will devise means to overcome individual
difficulties. Moreover I am equally certain that once keen on
netting you will want to examine every new and interesting
shopping bag or piece of netting to see how it has been made and
whether you can make one like it. Many of my friends have agreed
to their netted carriers being examined, partly undone and done up
again, but I have never yet stopped a complete stranger and asked
if I might see how her string bag was made. One can imagine the
misunderstandings.

Chapter 3
Beginners, please

The basic netting knot

This is like the Sheet Bend (in sailing) and the Weaver's Knot (in weaving and book-binding), but should be made as detailed below.

Required
2 pieces of string, preferably thick for easy handling, and about 18 inches long
A hook at a suitable height; that is about chest height.

1. With one piece make a closed loop by tying its two ends together. This will be used as a foundation loop. Hang it on the hook with the knot close to the hook (Fig. 4).

2. Using the second piece of string, pass all except the last two inches through the back of the foundation loop and hold at the intersection with the thumb and one finger of the left hand (Figs. 5 & 6).

The left hand maintains this position throughout the process of forming the knot, keeping a firm hold of the string and the foundation loop where they cross. At the same time the left hand maintains a firm tension on the work by pulling the foundation loop towards the chest.

Fig. 4

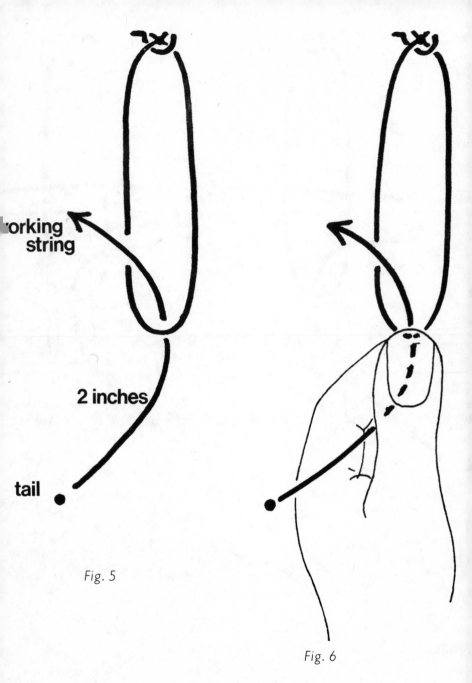

working
string

2 inches

tail

Fig. 5

Fig. 6

19

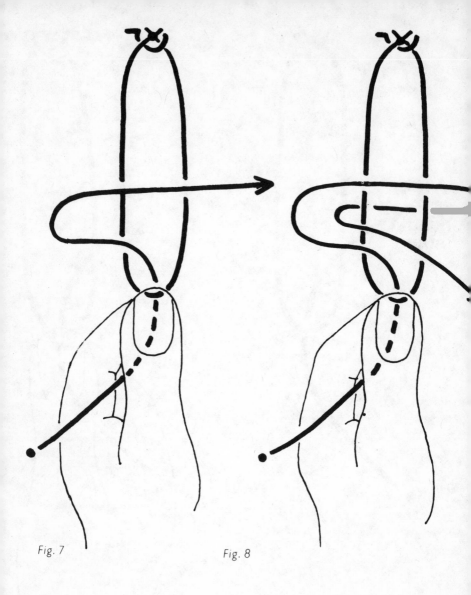

Fig. 7   Fig. 8

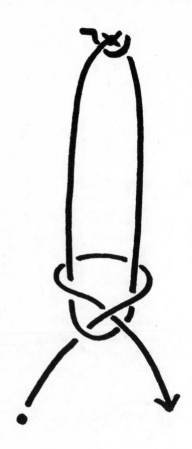

Fig. 9

3. Holding the long end of the string (the working end) in the right hand, throw an open loop over to the left. Take care not to allow a twist in this loop (Fig. 7).

4. With the right hand, take the end of the string to the right, round the back of the foundation loop and out to the front through the thrown loop (Figs. 8 & 9).

5. Keeping the left thumb and finger firmly in position until the last moment, pull the knot firm, but not tight at this stage.

correct   **incorrect**

Fig. 10

Note 1
Care must be taken to seat the knot correctly round the bottom of the foundation loop and not to let it slip below. The latter will slip and make a sloppy net, but the former will remain in position and make a firm net which will retain its shape.

With practice you will begin to manipulate the knot as you make it, holding, slackening and positioning as required with the thumb and finger of the left hand.

Note 2
Keep a steady tension on the whole piece throughout the process by pulling the work towards you with the left hand.

You have made your first netting knot!

Look at it proudly. Follow the line of the knot. Feel the flow. This is the basic knot with which all your nets will be made.

Undo the knot and repeat it until you feel really familiar with it. Try doing it with your eyes closed. When you feel happy with it, take out your medium netting needle and start on the next stage.

Loading the needle

The netting needle is a beautifully functional tool, designed to hold conveniently until required, and to serve easily when needed, as long a length of string as possible; for the fewer joining knots there are the better.

You will find it best to cut off a measured length of string before loading the needle, so that the twist produced as you load will run off at the free end. This will not be possible of course in the early stages when you do not know the capacity of the needles, so load direct from the ball in the first instance, cut off, unload the needle and measure the length of the string. Mark this by some permanent mark in the room and after this you can cut the required length of string to load the needle fully but without overloading and what is more the string can be laid out on the floor to untwist as you load.

The actual loading hardly needs any detailing as the needle is really simple.

1. Hold the needle in the left hand with the point upwards.

2. Hold the end of the string anywhere on the body of the needle with the left thumb.

a

Fig. 11

3. Run the string up the body, round the prong and down the same side of the body to trap the starting end of the string (Fig. 11a).

Note
The needle is flexible so by pressing on the point of the needle with the right hand the prong is left clear and the string can be run round it easily.

4. Take the string round the bottom or heel of the needle, between the two projections.

5. Turn the needle back to front, still with the point upwards, and continue loading by repeating the same processes:
(i)   up the body, round the prong and down the same side
(ii) under the heel, turn the needle, and up the other side
(iii) round the prong again and down the same side, etc.

6. Continue until the needle is comfortably loaded. Neither the prong nor the heel should be completely filled or the string will spill off. It will be obvious that in use an extra working length of string will be released from the needle by pulling back on the needle so that the working string presses on the flexible point and clears the prong (Fig. 11b).

b

Chapter 4
The course

A first practice piece

This is a simple piece of diamond mesh, straightforward and repetitive, requiring no new knots but reinforcing the formation of the newly learned netting knot and introducing the mesh stick. The piece itself is of no practical use and can be discarded (or proudly displayed as your first piece of netting; children will certainly wish to keep it). However the process is genuine and with more meshes per row would produce items such as hammocks, fruit nets, etc. Unfortunately to do this in any greater width calls for a different way of setting up and a new knot. This would be an unnecessary complication and has therefore been left until later. (See Chapter 4, A woollen scarf.)

Required

1 medium netting needle (about $\frac{3}{4}$ inch width)
1 mesh stick, $1\frac{1}{2}$ inch width
18 inches medium string (for the foundation loop)
6 yards medium string (to load the needle)

Be sure to use the sizes of needle and mesh stick specified. Remember the mesh stick sets the size of the mesh and must be comfortably wider than the needle to give ample room to pass your needle through the meshes as you work.

Casting on

1. Start as before with a foundation loop, made from your 18-inch piece, and hung on a hook in a suitable netting position.

2. Load the needle and attach the string as before to the bottom of the foundation loop with a netting knot.

3. Hold the mesh stick in the left hand. Hold it correctly from below with the thumb at the front (Fig. 12).

4. Lay the working string over the front of the mesh stick. At this point do not be concerned about the mesh stick being close up to the foundation loop (Fig. 13).

5. Take the string round below and up behind the mesh stick, and out through the foundation loop from the back (Fig. 14).

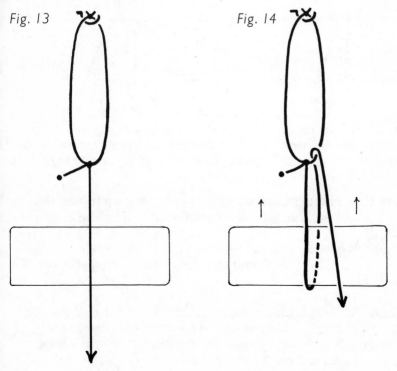

Fig. 12

Fig. 13

Fig. 14

6. Pull the needle downwards with your right hand and the mesh stick will be hauled by pulley effect to the bottom of the foundation loop (Fig. 15).

7. With the thumb and finger of the left hand hold the string *and* the foundation loop where they cross at the top of the mesh stick.

8. Form the knot and draw it firm but not tight. This is a wise precaution for beginners as it facilitates undoing if necessary (Fig. 16).

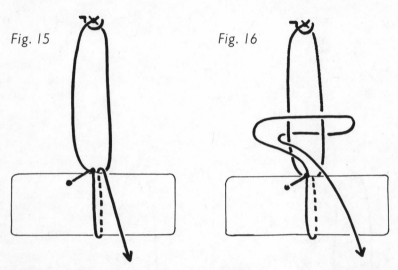

Fig. 15   Fig. 16

9. The mesh stick remains in position, encircled by this first loop and held in the left hand. The needle and the working string should be automatically *over* the front of the mesh stick and ready to continue by repeating the processes:

(i) Take the working string round the bottom and up behind the mesh stick, and out through the foundation loop from the back (Fig. 17).
(ii) Haul downwards with the right hand until the working string pulls the lower side of the foundation loop hard down on the top of the mesh stick.

Obviously the mesh stick cannot move, but be sure to pull down with the right hand so that the knot is always made close to the top of the mesh stick. Unless you do so, your meshes will not be uniform and your net will be badly shaped.

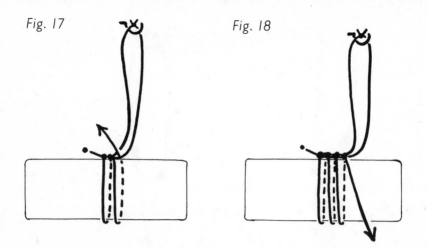

Fig. 17   Fig. 18

(iii) Hold the intersection with the left thumb at the front and the left index or second finger at the back.

Note
It will help in forming the knot if you can position your thumb to hold the intersection so that the working string can be thrown easily to the left; it is better to pinch finely with the tips of the thumb and finger rather than broadly with the thumb and finger flat.

(iv) Form the knot and pull firmly but not tightly, allowing the working string to ease down under the left thumb. It may be necessary to relax *slightly* the pressure of the left thumb to release the working string into position and then to re-apply the thumb pressure while you pull the knot firm. If the knot slips, do not despair; it needs practice.

10. Keeping the mesh stick in position with the left hand, repeat twice so that there are three loops on the mesh stick (Fig. 18). Do not count the knots at the top, but the bottom of the loops formed on the mesh stick.

The second row

1. Keep the foundation loop on its hook all the time. Remove the mesh stick. Pull on the needle with the right hand to apply a firm tension on the foundation loop. With the left hand, sort out the three newly made loops so that the last made loop is on the left ready to be used in the second row (Figs. 19 and 20).

29

Fig. 19 Fig. 20

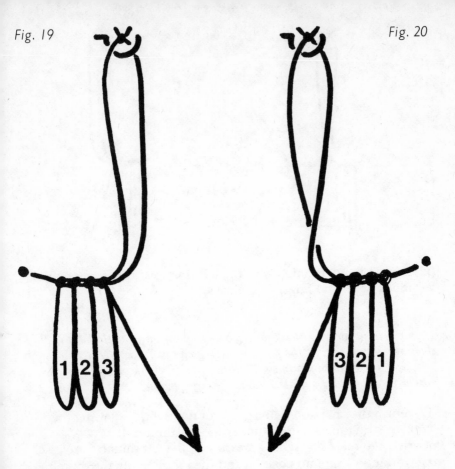

2. As before, lay the string over the front and round behind the mesh stick, and out through the *first* loop from the back.

3. Pull down on the needle and haul the mesh stick up to the bottom of the first loop.

4. Form the knot, but take care, for the danger here is that the beginner will tend to include in the knot the descending strand on the left as well as the two strands of the first loop.

To avoid taking in this extra strand, hold the intersection with the thumb and *second* finger of the left hand and use the left index finger to mark the space between the descending strand and the first loop, the space in fact through which your needle will pass as it comes round the back of the loop (Fig. 21).

Fig. 21

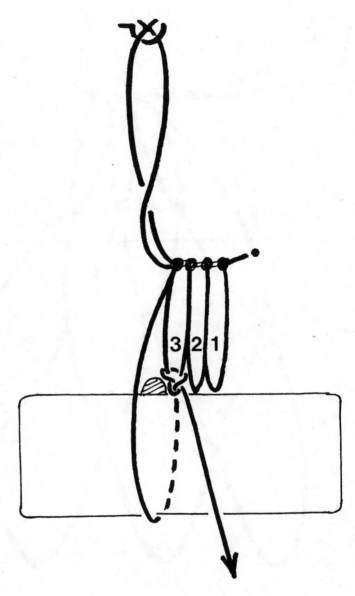

Note
This in fact makes the first full mesh. Up to now what have been called loops were in fact half-meshes.

5. The mesh stick remains in position and by repeating the same processes and meshing into loop 2 and loop 1, the second row will be completed with three full meshes.

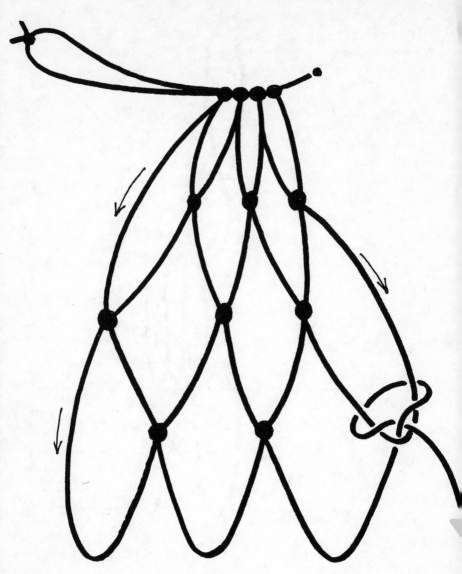

Fig. 22

The third and subsequent rows

1. Remove the mesh stick only at the end of each row and continue meshing successive rows, always working from left to right. The processes fall into a natural rhythm and it is useful, even desirable, to check your work at the end of each row. With children the young beginner is glad to offer the work for inspection at such intervals, especially as with increasing skill the intervals are manifestly becoming shorter each time.

2. Stop when you feel you have had sufficient practice and are ready to apply the processes to making the first article, the football or basketball carrier.

Plate 1
Football/Basketball carrier

A football or basketball carrier

Required

1 medium needle
2 7-yard lengths medium string (two loads for the medium needle)
4 feet thick string
2-inch mesh stick
1 button and about 6 inches of finer string for the toggle.

Casting on for a grommet start

Fig. 23

A grommet is a ring of string or rope. In some methods of
bag-making it is made separately, but in this case is an integral part
of the work (Fig. 23). The grommet forms the base on which the
bag is made by netting rows of circular netting, using the 'tail' to
carry the working string to the new level for the next round.

1. Run about 4 feet of string off the needle and form a slip knot at least 40 inches from the end of the string, but *make certain that the knot slides on the tail* and not on the working string (Fig. 24a).

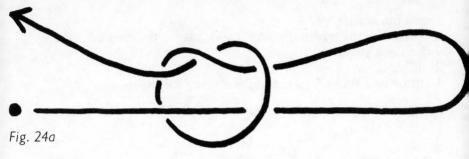

Fig. 24a

One method is to make a small loop by tucking the working string underneath, then pulling a small section of the tail through the first loop and making the resulting knot firm (Fig. 24b).

Fig. 24b

A quicker and amusing method (Fig. 25a) is to hold the needle in the left hand and place the first two fingers of the right hand with the thumb pointing to the right under the tail at least 40 inches from the end. Twist the tail into a loop by rolling the hand over so that the thumb now points to the left. With the two fingers grip the tail and by withdrawing the fingers from the first loop draw part of the tail through to make the slip knot (Fig. 25b).

2. Check that the knot slides on the tail. The tail should be at least 30 inches long and the loop above the slip knot 4 inches long; if not, pull out and re-tie correctly. It is good practice.

3. Hang the loop on a hook so that it can be used as a foundation loop in similar fashion to the first practice piece, except that this foundation loop is constructed so that it can be drawn up on the

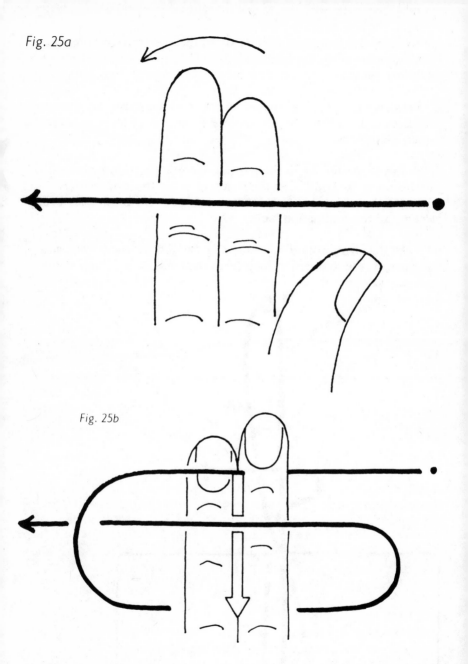

Fig. 25a

Fig. 25b

tail to make the grommet. Obviously in this case the working string is already part of the foundation loop and does not have to be tied on before starting.

4. See that the tail lies on the left of the working string. By the same processes used in the first practice piece, cast on 11 loops over the 2-inch mesh stick.

5. Hold the mesh stick in the left hand, correctly from below with the thumb at the front. Lay the string *over* the front of the mesh stick. (At this point do not be concerned about the mesh stick being close up to the foundation loop.)

6. Take the string round below and up behind the mesh stick and out through the foundation loop from the back.

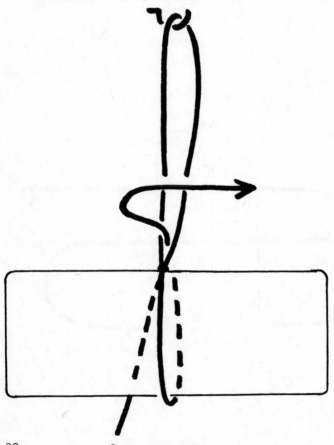

Fig. 26

7. Pull the needle downwards with the right hand and the mesh stick will be hauled by pulley effect hard up to the bottom of the foundation loop.

8. With the thumb and finger of the left hand, hold the working string and the foundation loop where they cross at the top of the mesh stick.

9. Form the netting knot by throwing a loop to the left and taking the needle to the right, then behind both strands of the foundation loop and out to the front through the thrown loop. Draw up the netting knot firm and neat but not fiercely tight for ease of pulling up later. Take care to form the knot close to the top of the mesh stick (Figs. 26 and 27).

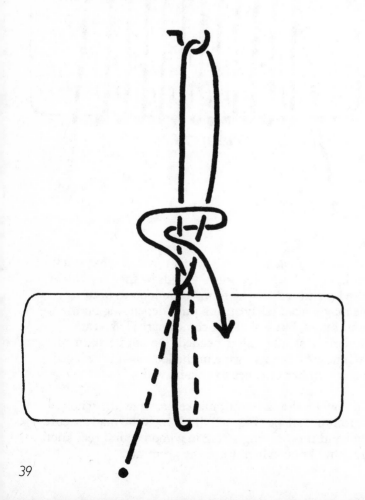

Fig. 27

10. Repeat 10 times to make 11 loops. You should count the loops at the bottom of the mesh stick and not at the top where there will be an extra knot (Fig. 28).

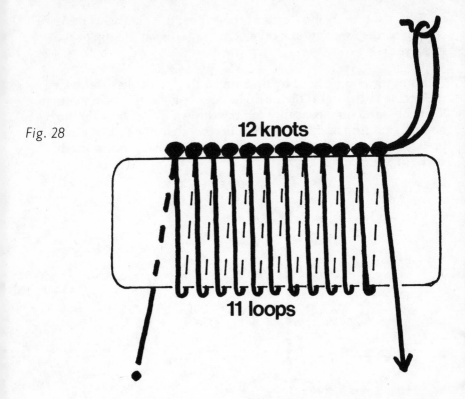

Fig. 28

12 knots

11 loops

11. Remove the mesh stick and tuck the tail through what is left of the foundation loop. Taking care not to withdraw the tail, pull at the point marked *a* and reduce the foundation loop to nothing (Fig. 29). This may need a fairly strong pull, depending on the tightness of your knots, but it will not come apart. Take care however not to jerk; a steady pull is needed. Do not be alarmed when a certain amount of twist forms in the loop as it is reduced. You can stop any number of times to ease it away.

12. By pulling now on the tail itself, marked *b*, draw the whole piece into its grommet shape (Fig. 30). This must be made secure by tying the tail and the working string in a good sound reef knot, close up to the other knots which form the grommet.

Fig. 29

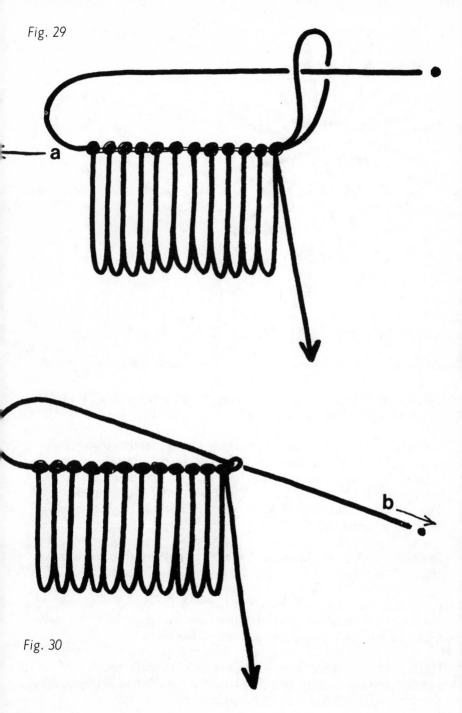

a

b

Fig. 30

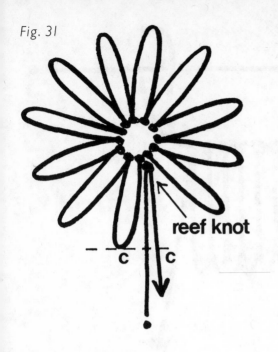

Fig. 31

reef knot

c   c

13. Now use the tail and the working string to make an additional (12th) loop the same size as all the other loops (Fig. 31).

To do this, lay the tail and the working string together alongside either of the neighboring loops and mark the point on them level with the base of the neighboring loop at *c*. At that point, tie the tail and the working string in a double overhand knot (Fig. 32). This is how the tail is used to carry the working string to the new level for the next row.

14. Make up the toggle by passing the finer string through two holes of the button and tying a reef knot below the button.

15. Thread the string of the toggle through the center of the grommet and hang the work on a hook by the toggle, so that it can rotate as you work round on each row (Fig. 33).

16. Place the working string on the right of the tail ready for meshing to the right. It may help at first to keep the tail out of the way by hitching it lightly to the hook.

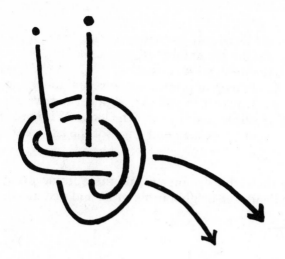

Fig. 32

Fig. 33

The first row

1. Mesh round in the usual way *but remove the mesh stick after every three meshes.* Do not try to force all the meshes of the complete circle on the mesh stick at once.
Take care to mesh each loop in proper sequence and to take any twist from the loops. It may help you as a beginner to have an assistant as a second pair of hands to sort the loops. With practice however you will begin to use a second finger of the left hand to do this for yourself.

2. After meshing the 11th loop, the tail and the working string must be measured with the neighbouring mesh and tied in a double overhand knot (Fig. 34).

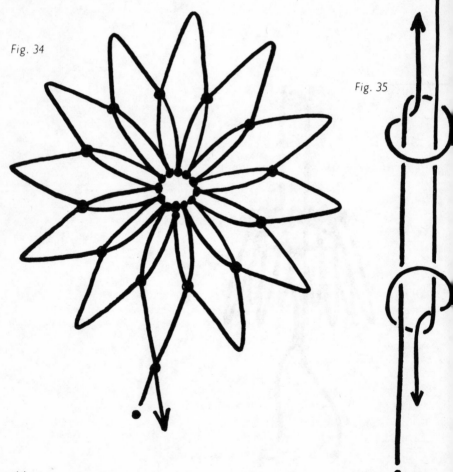

Fig. 34

Fig. 35

The second and subsequent rows

Continue meshing round, removing the mesh stick after every 3 meshes, and at the end of each row tying the tail and the working string in a double overhand knot.

As a check, count the meshes at the end of each round. If you have missed any meshes it will not need much taking back. There should of course be twelve meshes, including the last one made with the the double overhand knot.

Note on joining on a new length of string

After about 3 rows you will have used most of the string on the needle. To join on a new length of string, tie it on with any suitable knot, e.g. a reef knot. More sophisticated methods should be deferred until you are more accomplished.

Meanwhile a perfectly sound method, not too difficult and which appeals to children and adults, is the Fisherman's Knot (Fig. 35). This is made by making a simple overhand knot in each end round the other string. By pulling on the short ends you separate the knots and by pulling on the strings outside the knots you draw the two knots together into a firm Fisherman's Knot.

Alternatively you can use the same basic netting knot by turning back the last of the working string and making a netting knot in it with the new string (Fig. 36). This is in fact a Weaver's Knot and makes a sound joint. (For a speedier method of making this knot see Chapter 5, Now you can net.)

Finishing off

1. Complete 7 rows. (Count 7 rows of knots, excluding those of the grommet.) Tie off the last double overhand knot very firmly and cut off the ends neatly and fairly short.

2. Remove the toggle.

3. Lace the top round of meshes with the thick string for a draw string. A popular finish is made by tying the draw string in a double overhand knot, leaving both ends a good inch long (Fig. 37). Strand the two ends and separate the fibers in each strand with an ordinary hair comb. This makes a convincing tassel.

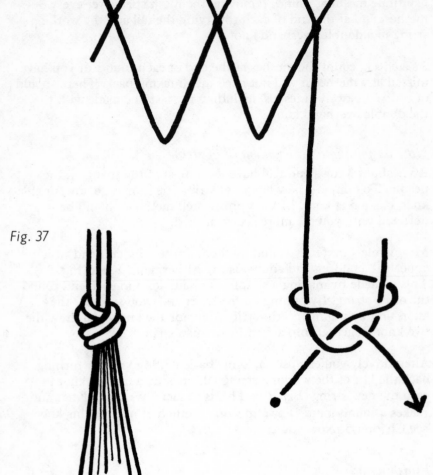

Fig. 36

Fig. 37

Alternative finish

1. After completing only 6 rows, make the double overhand knot with the tail and the working string and cut off the remainder of both.

2. Unload the string remaining on the needle and reload it double, that is, find the middle of the string and hook the middle over the prong of the needle. Lay both strands of the string together and load up the needle so that it will now serve double string (Fig. 38).

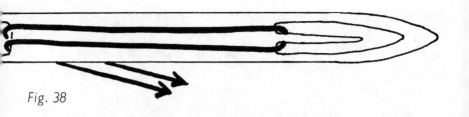

Fig. 38

3. Tie the double string with the usual netting knot to the bottom of any mesh other than the last one with its double overhand knot and complete one round of double meshes over the 2-inch mesh stick.

4. At the end of the round finish off with a netting knot on top of the starting knot.

5. Thread these double meshes with the draw string.

Plate 2   Shopping bag
with cane handles
with bottle bag in front

A bottle bag

This is a quick exercise with two functions; it is a quick repeat of a bag in circular netting to reinforce what you have learned already and at the same time it provides a quick bag on which to introduce handle making. Nonetheless it is a useful article and will in fact carry a large soda bottle or a full size bottle of wine.

Required

1 medium needle ($\frac{3}{4}$ inches wide)
2 7-yard lengths medium string
2-inch mesh stick
Button toggle
2 S-shaped hooks.

Casting on

1. The bag is made by the same method as the football or netball carrier. Make the 4-inch loop to slide on a 30-inch tail for a grommet start.

2. Cast on 7 loops and make the grommet:

(i)   tuck the tail through the loop
(ii) reduce the loop to nothing
(iii) pull the line of loops into a circle
(iv) secure this with a reef knot tied with the tail and the working string
(v)   make the extra (8th) loop equal in size to the neighboring loops with a double overhand knot with the tail and the working string.

3. Thread the button toggle through the grommet and hang it on a hook.

4. Mesh round for 6 rows, finishing each round with the usual double overhand knot in the tail and the working string. It will be appreciated by now that the function of this knot is conveyed by the name of 'drop knot', dropping as it does the working string to the required level for the next round.

Remember to remove the mesh stick after three meshes. Remember also to count the meshes at the end of each round to be sure you have missed no meshes.

5. After the last double overhand or drop knot, which must be particularly firm, cut off *only the tail* but leave the working string attached. This will be used to start the handle.

Handles

These are made by catching up a quarter of the meshes (in this case 2 meshes) for each end of a handle and thickening them and binding them together with half-hitching.

Two S-shaped hooks will be useful for this part of the work when rigged between two chair backs. They are not essential; two people can work together to provide the extra pair of hands required, but hooks enable the netter to be independent. As an alternative to hooks the work can be tied with short pieces of string to chair backs or other suitable holders.

The first handle

1. Leave the toggle in place and hang it with one S-hook to a chair back. Have the other S-hook ready on another chair back (Fig. 39). If not using S-hooks or string, leave the toggle in place on the hook used for netting and a second person can lend a finger to form the handle round.

Fig. 39

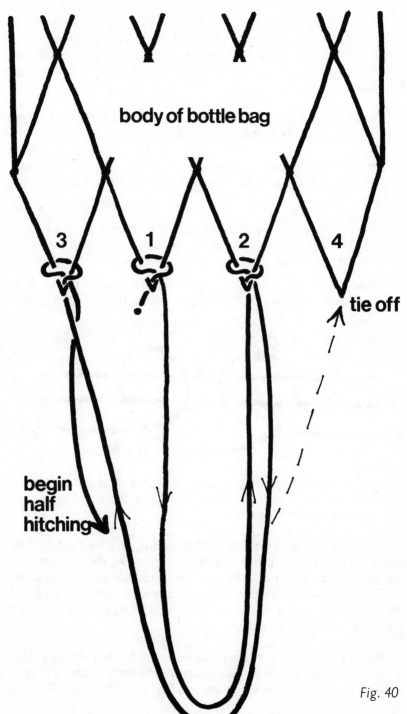

body of bottle bag

3

1

2

4

tie off

begin
half
hitching

Fig. 40

2. Consider the 8 meshes in two halves; 4 neighboring meshes are to be used for each handle (Fig. 40). Take the string already attached to the last drop knot round the second hook or finger at a suitable distance to make a reasonable sized handle (e.g. about 6 inches).

3. Take the string through the next mesh to the right of the drop knot and fasten it there with a netting knot.

4. Return the string round the hook again and through the next mesh to the left of the drop knot and fasten it there with a netting knot.

5. This time instead of returning the string round the hook, begin half-hitching about half-way up the handle. The half-hitching is made in an alternately over and under process:

(i)   take the working string *over* and right round the two strands of the handle and under the working string itself (Fig. 41). Pull tight.

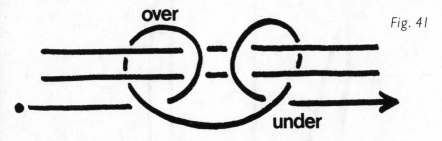

over

Fig. 41

under

(ii) take the working string *under* and right round the two strands and under the working string itself. Pull tight and close up to the previous half-hitch.

Continue alternately over and under, easing each half-hitch close up to the previous one and taking care to seat all the hitching neatly in a straight line on the outside of the handle. It will form itself into a natural curve to make a decorative handle (Fig. 42). It helps to avoid mistakes if you *audibly* say 'over' and 'under' as you begin each half-hitch.

6. When the hitching works up close to the hook, re-arrange the hooks so that the hitching can be done between the hooks (Fig. 43). Again when convenience demands it, revert to the original

52

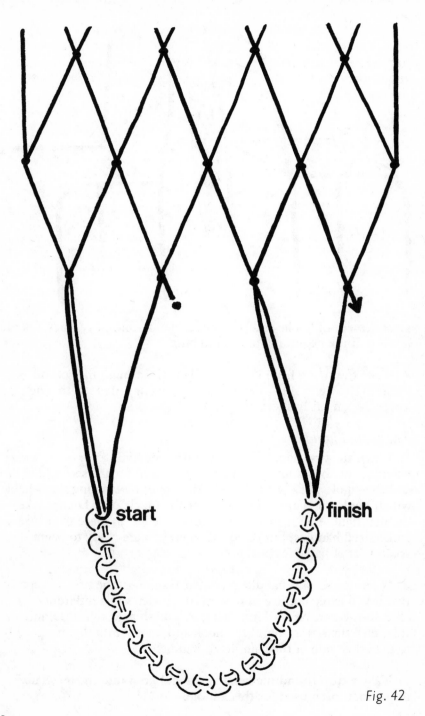

start

finish

Fig. 42

Fig. 43

arrangement of hooks and continue hitching until it reaches a point level with the beginning of the hitching.

7. Take the string from the last half-hitch through the second mesh to the right of the drop knot and fasten it there with a netting knot. Cut off fairly short.

The second handle

1. When the first handle is finished, the remaining 4 meshes hang down below the handle. These are to be used for the second handle and the whole work needs to be turned over by twisting the S-hook which holds the handle. Do not alter the toggle end. Do not take the first handle off its hook; this should be left in place to ensure equal sized handles, but removed when you are ready to begin the second set of half-hitching.

2. Work the second handle in similar fashion to the first, except that it will avoid confusion to work the meshes in a different order (Fig. 44). Knot the working string to a mesh next to the completed side, take the string round the hook and knot it into the mesh next to the other side of the completed handle.

3. Take a turn round the hook again and knot into the mesh next to the first mesh used for this handle.

54

Fig. 44

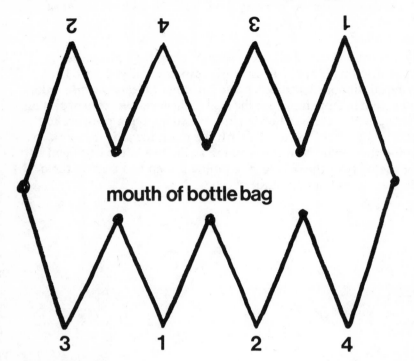

second handle

first handle

4. Complete the half-hitching so that it is the same length as that on the first handle and fasten off in the only remaining mesh.

Note
(i)   *The order of meshing on the first handle is 3, 1, 2, 4, i.e. working outwards from the middle.*
(ii) *The order of meshing on the second handle is 1, 3, 4, 2, i.e. inwards towards the middle.*

   Obviously there are other ways of doing this, but I recommend that you establish this principle so that when used later with the complication of far more meshes you will avoid the disappointment and tedium of meshes missed or taken in the wrong order.
(iii) *You will find the half-hitching easier if you work from left to right and if you follow the meshing order this will happen. Working from left to right enables you to use the left hand to hold the working strand away from the double strands of the handle,*

while the right hand takes the needle over or under the two strands and easily under the working string held out with the left hand.

Fingers sore?

At this point you may find the working string has been pressing into the first finger or the little finger, especially if you have been working continuously through these patterns. To ease the discomfort or to prevent it happening, use the heel of the needle instead of pulling the string with your hand or fingers. When applying pressure to tighten a knot, hold the needle with the point towards the work, grasping the needle with the working string inside the hand and along the body of the needle; the pull will then be taken on the heel of the needle and not on tender flesh.

A shaped single-color shopping bag

Fig. 45

57

This bag is made on the same principle as the bottle bag, but introduces increasings to give the bag more shape and greater capacity. As explained in the introduction, this is a basic pattern which can be enlarged and developed to suit different requirements.

Required

1 fine needle ($\frac{1}{2}$ inch wide)
1 medium needle ($\frac{3}{4}$ inch wide)
1-inch mesh stick
2-inch mesh stick
1 button toggle
2 S-shaped hooks
5 4-yard lengths of colored medium string, for use with the fine needle to work in the small 'increase' meshes when making the body of the bag
8 yards of the same string for use with the medium needle and the 2-inch mesh stick to make the double row
2 6-yard lengths of the same string for the two handles.

Casting on

1. With a fine needle loaded with 4 yards of the string, form the slip knot with a 4-inch loop and a 30-inch tail for a grommet start.
2. Cast on 11 loops over the 1-inch mesh stick.
3. Draw up into a grommet and secure with a reef knot.
4. Tie the tail and the working string in a double overhand knot to make the 12th loop the same size as the other 11 loops.

5. Thread the button toggle through the grommet and hang on a hook at a suitable height for netting.

6. With the 1-inch mesh stick, mesh all the way round in plain netting, that is with no increases yet, and tie off the tail and the working string in the usual double overhand knot. Count the meshes and check that there are 12.

Note
In working the plain rounds, remember to remove the mesh stick after each three or four meshes.

The first increasing round (12 meshes become 16)

1. Mesh in the ordinary way into the first mesh.

2. Increase by meshing again *into the same mesh* (Fig. 46).

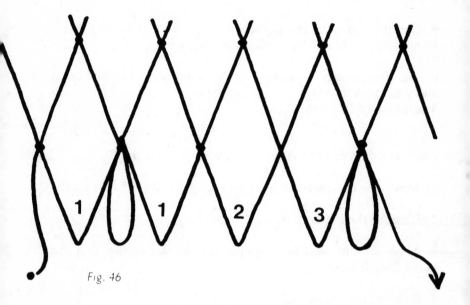

Fig. 46

3. Remove the mesh stick.

4. Mesh in the ordinary way into the next three meshes.

5. Increase by meshing again into the same 3rd mesh.

6. Remove the mesh stick.

Note
In the increasing rounds, removing the mesh stick after an increase is a reminder to make the increase and so avoid having to undo work and go back to make the increase in the correct place.

7. Complete the round by meshing three and increasing in the 3rd mesh each time.

59

8. After the 4th increase, do not be alarmed that you have only one more mesh to work. When this one has been worked and you have made the usual double overhand knot with the tail and the working string, these two loops together with the first mesh at the beginning of the round will complete the pattern of 'three and increase'.

9. Count the meshes in the complete round to check that there are 16 meshes including the small increase loops.

10. Mesh a plain round, that is with no increases, but make certain that you mesh into all loops *including the small increase loops*. Check that there are 16 meshes.

The second increasing round (16 meshes become 20)

1. Mesh one and increase by meshing again into the first mesh.

2. Remove the mesh stick.

3. Mesh into the next *four* meshes and increase by meshing again in the fourth mesh.

4. Remove the mesh stick.

5. Complete the round by meshing 4 and increasing in the 4th mesh each time. Remove the mesh stick after each increase.

6. After increasing for the 4th time in this round, you will need only to mesh two. Make the usual double overhand knot with the tail and the working string, and the pattern of 'four and increase' will be complete with the first mesh of the round.

7. Count the meshes in the complete round to check that there are 20 meshes including the small increase loops.

8. Mesh a plain round, no increases, making certain that you mesh into all loops including the small increase loops. Check that there are 20 meshes.

The third increasing round (20 meshes become 24)

1. Mesh one and increase in the same mesh.

2. Remove the mesh stick.

3. Mesh 5 and increase in the 5th mesh.

4. Remove the mesh stick.

5. Complete the round by meshing 5 and increasing in the 5th mesh each time.

6. After the 4th increase, there will be three meshes, the double overhand knot and the starting mesh to complete the pattern of five.

7. Count to check that there are 24 meshes including the increases.

8. Mesh a plain round, making sure that all loops including the increases are meshed. Check that there are 24 meshes.

9. Mesh two more plain rounds and at the end of each check that there are 24 meshes.

The double row with the 2-inch mesh

1. Cut off the tail and the working string fairly close.

2. Find the middle of the 8-yard length of string, hang it over the prong of the medium needle and load up with double string. (See the alternative finish to the football or basketball carrier.)

3. Using the netting knot, fasten the double string to the bottom of any mesh other than the last mesh made with the double overhand knot.

4. Using the 2-inch mesh stick, mesh one round in double string.

5. At the end of the round, finish off by knotting on top of the starting knot.

6. Firm the last knot and cut off the double string fairly close.

The handles

The handles are made in the same way as those of the bottle bag, except that as there are many more meshes some are knotted together to reduce the number of side strings. This is not absolutely essential and may become one of your variants in later use of the pattern, but remember that with an increased number of side strings you will need more than the 6 yards of string specified in this pattern for each handle.

Compare the process in making the handles for the bottle bag, particularly the order of working the meshes, outwards for the first handle and inwards for the second.

The first handle

1. Leave the toggle in the grommet and hang it with one of the S-hooks to a chair back. Have the other S-hook ready on another chair back.

2. Load one of the 6-yard lengths of string on the medium needle.

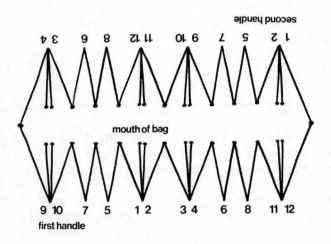

Fig. 47

3. Attach the string by tying together with a netting knot any two neighboring meshes (Nos. 1 and 2).

4. Run the string from these two meshes, round the second S-hook to make a 6-inch handle.

62

5. Take the string through the next two meshes to the right of the first two tied together. Tie these two meshes together with a netting knot (Nos. 3 and 4).

6. Take the string back again round the S-hook and knot it to the next mesh to the left of the start of the handle (No. 5).

7. Return over the S-hook and knot into the mesh to the right of Nos. 3 and 4 (No. 6).

8. Return over the S-hook and knot into the mesh to the left of No. 5 (No. 7).

9. Return over the S-hook and knot into the mesh to the right of No. 6 (No. 8).

10. Return over the S-hook and knot into the *two* meshes to the left of No. 7 (Nos. 9 and 10).

11. This time instead of returning over the S-hook, begin alternate half-hitching halfway up the handle and continue until both sides balance.

12. Finish off the first handle by tying off the string by knotting together the two meshes to the right of No. 8 (Nos. 11 and 12).

13. Cut off the remaining string fairly close.

The second handle
When the first handle is finished, the remaining twelve meshes will be hanging down below the first handle. These are to be used for the second handle and must be brought to the top above the finished handle. To do this, leave the toggle where it is and turn the whole work by twisting the S-hook which holds the first handle. Do not take the first handle off its hook; this should be left in place to ensure equal sized handles, but removed when you are ready to begin the second set of half-hitching.

Reload the medium needle with the other 6 yards of string. Work the second handle in similar fashion except that you will work the meshes in reverse order.

1. Attach the string with a netting knot to the two unworked

meshes next to the finish of the first handle (Nos. 1 and 2).

2. Take the string round the S-hook and fasten it with one netting knot to the bottom of the two unworked meshes next to the other end of the first handle (Nos. 3 and 4).

3. Take the string round the S-hook each time and fasten side strings to each mesh in turn following the numberings (5, 6, 7, 8 singly and 9 and 10 together).

4. Begin alternate half-hitching, comparing the first handle before removing it from the S-hook.

5. Continue alternate half-hitching until both sides balance.

6. Finish off the second handle by knotting together the remaining two unworked meshes with the end of the 6 yard string.

7. Cut off fairly close.

A shaped shopping bag in two colors

This is the same pattern as the single color shopping bag, but with one difference; instead of the usual 'tail', a second working string is used and each one acts alternately as the tail to bring the other colored string to the next level.

'Bosun's Plait' is introduced as an alternative method of finishing the handles.

Plate 3   On the left, a shopping bag with 'Bosun's Plait' handles and on the right one with cane handles

Required
2 fine needles ($\frac{1}{2}$ inch wide)
2 medium needles ($\frac{3}{4}$ inch wide)

1-inch mesh stick
2-inch mesh stick
Button toggle
2 S-hooks
2 5-yard lengths of medium string in *each* color for use with the
fine needles to make the body of the bag
4 yards of medium string of *each* color for use with the medium
needles and the 2-inch mesh stick for the double row
6 yards of medium string in the lighter color for the side strings
2 3-yard lengths of medium string in the darker color for finishing
the handles in Bosun's Plait.

Casting on

1. With a fine needle loaded with 5 yards of the darker string, cast
on 11 loops over the 1-inch mesh stick as in the previous pattern,
except that the tail need only be short, say 6 inches.

2. Draw up the grommet, secure it with a reef knot and make the
12th loop the same size as the other 11 loops, using a double
overhand knot with the tail and the working string.

Note
*It will be clear that the function of the tail in circular netting is to
lower the working string to the next working level and that it is made
as an extra mesh with the working string in the double overhand knot.
It will be simpler if from now on I give this knot its functional name
and refer to it as the 'drop knot'.*

3. Cut off the tail fairly close.

4. With a fine needle loaded with 5 yards of the lighter string,
attach the new string to the bottom of the last mesh by tying a
netting knot directly above the 'drop knot' (Fig. 48).

5. Cut off the short end of the light string fairly close like the dark
tail.

6. Leave the dark string hanging as a tail and mesh one plain
round, that is with no increases, in the light string.

7. Make the drop knot at the end of the round with the two
different colored strings.

8. Check that there are 12 meshes.

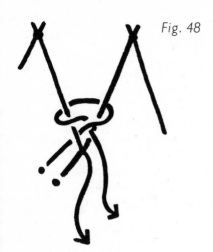

Fig. 48

The first increasing round with the dark string
(12 meshes become 16)

1. Leave the light string hanging as a tail and work with the dark string for the increasing round.

2. Mesh into the first mesh in the usual way and increase by meshing again into the same mesh.

3. Remove the mesh stick.

4. Mesh into the next three meshes and increase by meshing again into the 3rd mesh.

5. Remove the mesh stick as a reminder in this round to count three meshes and then increase.

6. Remember that after the 4th increase in this round you will have *one* mesh and the drop knot to go with the first mesh of the round to complete the pattern of 'three and increase'.

7. Tie the drop knot with the two working strings of different colours.

8. Count the meshes in the complete round to check that there are 16 meshes including the small increase loops.

A plain round in the light string

1. Leave the dark string hanging as a tail.

2. Using the light string, mesh a plain round, no increases, but make certain that you mesh into all the loops, including the small increase loops.

3. Check that there are 16 loops.

4. It will be obvious that the darker color will continue to make the increasing rounds and the lighter color the plain rounds, so working with alternate colors and leaving the idling color as the tail, continue as in the previous pattern.

5. Mesh one and increase; mesh four and increase in each 4th, finishing the round with mesh 2 and the drop knot (20 meshes).

6. Mesh a plain round (20 meshes).

7. Mesh one and increase; mesh five and increase in each 5th, finishing the round with mesh three and the drop knot (24 meshes).

8. Mesh three plain rounds in alternate colors, light, dark, light (24 meshes).

9. Cut off both colors fairly close.

The double row with the 2-inch mesh stick

1. Load the medium needle double with 4 yards of each color.

2. Attach the double string with a netting knot to the bottom of any mesh other than the finish and mesh round without increase over the 2-inch mesh stick.

3. Finish off with a netting knot directly above the starting knot.

4. Cut off both colors fairly close.

Handles

The handles can be done by the same method as in the shaped single color bag, that is in alternate half-hitching, but with variations in colors, e.g. light side strings and dark half-hitching or light side strings and light half-hitching on one handle and the reverse on the other. You will of course need different amounts of string from those shown for the handles at the head of this pattern. Allow 6 yards of string for each handle with half-hitching.

A particular kind of braiding, known as 'Bosun's Plait', will be familiar to many people from decorative lanyards. It is very effective in two colors, makes excellent handles and is easy to do and intriguing to children and adults (Fig. 49).

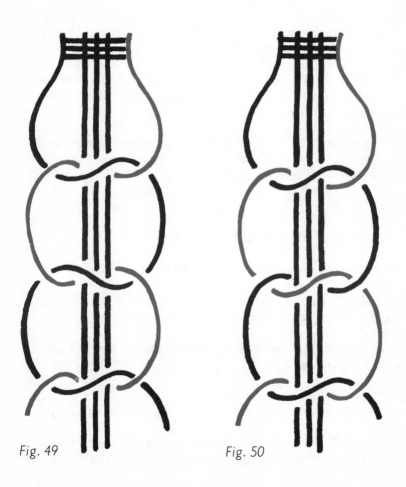

Fig. 49   Fig. 50

Handles in Bosun's Plait

As in the single color shopping bag, use S-hooks etc. and make the side strings in the same way, except for one difference; instead of leaving meshes 11 and 12 (Fig. 47) without a side string until the handle has been thickened, in this case complete the side stringing, including meshes 11 and 12. With the side strings thus completed, they can be thickened with the new braiding.

2. Re-arrange the S-hooks to stretch the side strings as when making the handles in half-hitching the work becomes too close to the hook for convenience (Fig. 43).

3. Find the middle of one of the 3-yard lengths of the dark string and tie it round the side strings about halfway up the handle with a suitable knot. An overhand knot will do, but it is possible by referring to the later chapter on knots to use a clove hitch or better still a constrictor knot. This is a matter of choice and if preferred the more suitable knots can wait.

4. If you have middled your 3 yards of string properly the ends will be of equal length. It is as well to check that they are for it is very annoying to have your string run short on one side before you have finished whilst you still have an unusable abundance on the other side.

5. Be sure you tie in all the side strings and no others.

6. (a) Lay the left hand string over the side strings, leaving a loop on the left.
(b) Take the right hand string over the end of the left hand string, under the side strings and out through the loop left in the left hand string.
(c) Pull tight and evenly on both strings, making the pull at right angles to the side strings.

7. Repeat 6(a), (b) and (c) in reverse, i.e.
(a) Lay the right hand string over the side strings, leaving a loop to the right.
(b) Take the left hand string over the end of the right hand string, under the side strings and out through the loop left in the right hand string.
(c) Pull tight and evenly on both strings, making the pull at right angles to the side strings.

8. Continue by repeating alternately 6(a), (b) and (c) and 7(a), (b) and (c) until both sides balance.

9. Thread back the loose ends and cut off close. A tapestry needle is particularly useful for this because of its blunt point and its generous eye. Failing this a blunted darning or crewel needle will suffice.

Note 1
In estimating the amount of string required for Bosun's Plait it is as well to allow string equal to 18 to 20 times the length of braiding required. The amount will obviously be affected by the thickness of the core being braided.

Note 2
If you braid consistently with either 6(a), (b), (c) or 7(a), (b), (c), that is without alternating, the plait will form itself in an interesting spiral, known appropriately as 'Rolling Bosun' (Fig. 50).
Obviously a consistent right hand lead will roll the Bosun one way and a consistent left hand lead the other. 'Rolling Bosun' does not make a comfortable handle, but it is as well to be aware of it as a possibility if only to diagnose the fault if your intended Bosun's Plait shows signs of rolling.

Note 3
A particularly charming two color effect can be made by using two 1½-yard lengths of string of different colors. In this case you could not start with an overhand knot or a clove hitch etc., but you would simply secure the two separate strands to the side strings with a temporary lashing and later when the braiding was complete remove the temporary fastening and thread the strands back at this end the same as at the finishing end.

A woollen scarf in diamond mesh

This pattern makes an attractive scarf which is very warm and comfortable to wear. It is an interesting change to work in a different material. The scarf is simple to make and popular with boys as well as girls.

Plate   A diamond mesh woollen scarf

It consists of a strip of plain diamond mesh netting and provides the opportunity to introduce a standard method of casting on plain netting. This is done by forming a first row of half-meshes with clove hitches on a headrope (Fig. 51). After netting a few rows the headrope can be withdrawn and the clove hitches fall out leaving slightly oversize meshes. With thin string for a headrope, the discrepancy is negligible.

Fig. 51

When working with wool, care must be taken not to pull too hard and stretch the wool or the netting will lose shape; knots are difficult to undo so you should avoid mistakes which will require the work being taken back.

Required
2 ozs. double knitting wool
1-inch mesh stick
1 medium needle
A short length of fine string for casting on.

Casting on
1. Take about 14 yards of wool, middle it and load the needle double by first hooking the middle of the wool over the prong of the needle. This loop in the middle of the 14 yards will become the end of the first working length and will be useful for joining on a new length of wool.

2. For casting on, tie the short length of fine string as a headrope between two suitable points, e.g. two chair backs or either side of one open backed chair. It is wise not to make the headrope too tight for some play is needed when making the clove hitches and holding the mesh stick in position.

3. Attach the double wool to the left end of the headrope with a clove hitch.

4. Cast on 15 loops or half meshes over the 1-inch mesh stick, attaching each half mesh to the headrope with a clove hitch.

5. While the work is still attached to the headrope it will not be

possible to reverse the netting to work from left to right except by moving yourself and working from the opposite side of the headrope.

6. Mesh for about 5 rows over the 1-inch mesh stick. Take care not to include in the first knot of each row the descending string from the previous row. (See again, A first practice piece, on page 30.)

7. To make it possible to reverse the work and so obviate moving from one side to the other, after about 5 rows remove the headrope from the chair back or its other supports, withdraw it from the clove hitches, which will now fall out; instead thread it through the first row of meshes, tie it in a loop and hang it on a suitable hook. The work will now hang free to rotate and you will be able to work easily from left to right on each row. Obviously the string can be threaded through any row of meshes and later as the scarf grows the work can be shortened for ease of working, if for instance you wish to work with a foot loop instead of from a hook and the scarf is so long that the netting is too close for comfortable working.

8. At the end of a length of wool, you will be left with the loop which was hung over the prong of the needle. The new length can be attached with a netting knot by using the loop like a mesh.

9. After about 45 rows you should still have enough wool left to make 30 tassels in double wool. In case of doubt, cut off sufficient pieces for the tassels and continue netting with peace of mind.

Tassels

Two pieces of wool 4 to $4\frac{1}{2}$ inches long, are required for the bottom of each mesh at each end of the scarf. The tassels are made by middling two of the pieces of wool, looping them over the bottom of an end mesh and pulling the open ends through their own middles. Pull each tassel firm and see that their ends are even. Trim if necessary (Fig. 52).

Note

An interesting effect is possible by using 1 ounce each of two different coloured wools and loading the needle double with equal lengths of each so that each mesh is made with the two colors side by side.

Fig. 52

A shopping bag
with cane or loop handles

This is a most capacious bag, very easily netted but needing a little ingenuity in setting up and finishing off. It is not however beyond the ability of adults or children who have reached this level of skill in netting. It can be regarded as an extra in the course or as a finishing piece for the really proficient.

The bag is made of a straight piece of flat diamond mesh netting like the scarf, but attached at each end to ready-made handles. The netting at this point looks like a miniature hammock and is made into a bag by folding the netting over with handles together and gathering up and securing the sides.

Plate 5   Various types of handle finishes. Top left: Bosun's Plait. Bottom left half-hitching. Bottom right: cane

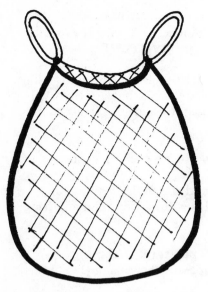

Fig. 53

A reasonable sized bag can be made with 25 rows of netting, but 35 rows makes a really ample size.

Required

1 medium needle
2-inch mesh stick for starting the casting on and off processes
1-inch mesh stick for the body of the bag
2 handles in cane or looped rope
16 4-yard lengths of fine to medium string (for 25 rows)
16 5½-yard lengths of fine to medium string (for 35 rows).

Note
Fine rather than thicker string is more suitable for this bag as it hangs better and is less bulky.

Handles

Suitable cane handles, 4 inches diameter, can be bought from suppliers of craft materials or can be made by softening fairly thick basketry cane by soaking in water and forming it into a circle and twisting the ends over and over as in making a rope grommet (compare Fig. 65).

Alternatively handles can be made out of rope of suitable thickness, e.g. domestic clothes line made out of cotton or plastic covered cord). A piece about 18 inches long can be made into a circle by overlapping the two ends for about 3 inches and tying the overlap securely with fine string or splicing it properly (see Fig. 66).

1. Hang one of the handles on a hook suitable for netting. If using cane handles, do not hang them directly on the hook or they will bruise and be badly marked; hang them by a loop of string to the hook.

2. Load the medium needle with one 16-yard length of string.

3. Allow a tail of at least 48 inches and attach the string to the handle with a clove hitch. If the tail is a nuisance, coil it and hang it on the hook out of the way.

4. Make the clove hitch tight and to prevent it slackening and slipping, 'crown' it by adding a simple overhand knot (Fig. 54).

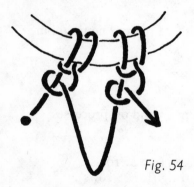

Fig. 54

5. It will give a neater finish if you cover the splice or joint in the handle, so position your first clove hitch so that succeeding ones cover that part of the handle.

6. Make one loop over the 2-inch mesh stick and tie it securely to the handle with another crowned clove hitch.

7. It is very awkward doing this with the mesh stick in position, especially with a cane handle, which is less yielding than the headrope used for casting on the woollen scarf, so having established the size of the first loop, you can dispense with the mesh stick and by using your fingers make all succeeding loops the same size as the first. Simply place the second or third finger of the left hand in the first loop instead of the mesh stick and form all

subsequent loops over that finger, leaving the left thumb and index finger free to help in forming the clove hitch and its crowning knot. When a number of knots have been formed like this and the finger becomes crowded, slip them off and re-insert the finger in the last loop and continue using that loop as the gauge. Clear the finger and change to another last loop as often as necessary.

8. Continue in this fashion until you have cast on 25 loops. For a good satisfying finish position each clove hitch neatly, close to its neighbor and with all the crowning knots in line.

9. The handle is free to rotate so each row can be worked from left to right merely by turning the work from back to front.

10. Continue meshing each row from left to right, but take care not to include in the first knot of each row the descending strand from the previous row. (See again, A first practice piece, on page 30.)

11. Mesh for 25 or 35 rows according to the size of bag required. You can form a reasonable idea of the size of the finished bag any number of rows will produce by folding the netting so that the bottom of the last row of meshes is level with the bottom of the 2-inch loops of the casting on row and loosely gathering up the sides into a bag shape. Whatever number of rows you decide on, see that it is an odd number and your finishing off will be simpler.

Casting off
1. To cast off, move the handle from the hook and hang it by its loop on a chair back and hang the second handle similarly on another chair back. Position the two chairs so that the working string will comfortably reach the second handle.

2. With the 2-inch mesh stick, measure on the working string a point 2 inches beyond the bottom of the last mesh and attach the working string at this point to the second handle with a crowned clove hitch. This will give you the start of a row of 2-inch casting off loops similar to the casting on loops at the beginning.

3. Remember you will wish to cover the joint in the handle so position your first knot appropriately.

4. The mesh stick will be awkward at this stage and can be

dispensed with. From now on you will be able to gauge the length of loop by eye and by the feel of the work.

5. Mesh with an ordinary netting knot into the first mesh.

6. Make a crowned clove hitch on the handle, close up to the first one, pulling the netting reasonably taut between the two chairs.

7. Continue alternately with (5) and (6) until you have attached all meshes to the handle, finishing off with the working string attached by a clove hitch to the handle. You will be constantly changing position between the chairs, first facing the finishing handle to make a crowned clove hitch, then facing the last row of meshes to make a netting knot.

8. Leave a tail of at least 48 inches and cut off.

9. The tails will be on opposite sides of the netting and are to be used to lace each side for gathering (Fig. 55).

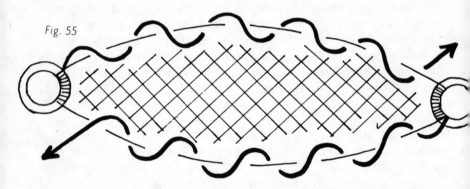

Fig. 55

10. Thread the tails through the side meshes on their respective sides and through the handle at the opposite end.

11. Draw up one side to 9 or 10 inches by pulling on the tail and tying it with a crowned clove hitch to the opposite handle.

12. Do the same with the other side. The length of the side string determines the size of the opening or mouth of the bag and you might like to draw up and tie both the side strings temporarily to check for size and then adjust if necessary. In either case, be sure

to secure both sides properly after deciding on the size.

13. The remainder of the tails will provide a string at each side already anchored for securing and reinforcing the side meshes.

14. With these side strings work down each side making a simple overhand knot over each side mesh (Fig. 56). You might find it a help to fix the middle side mesh at each side with a temporary lashing so that the meshes can be balanced fairly evenly either side of the middle. If possible, arrange the spacing of the side meshes more closely near the middle and less closely near the handles (Fig. 57).

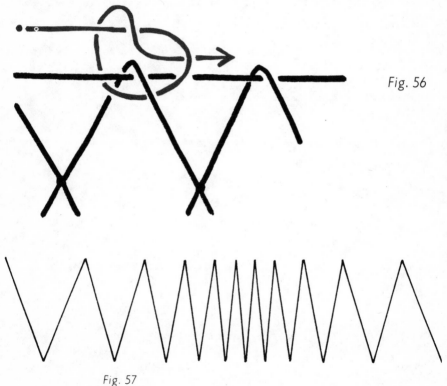

Fig. 56

Fig. 57

15. After the last side mesh has been secured, tie off the side strings with crowned clove hitches to the appropriate handle and cut off fairly close. For neatness the ends can be darned back under the hitching on the handles.

Chapter 5
Now you can net
–General hints and further work

As an accomplished netter, you are quite capable of operating on your own. You will now vary, especially by enlarging, the patterns which make up the course laid out in Chapter 4. You will also discover different patterns or invent completely new ones. Later in this section, there are a number of more ambitious items, like the hammock, which will tempt the keen netter. Meanwhile there are some suggestions and refinements of technique which will be useful to the able netter but which could not be introduced earlier without the risk of confusing or overwhelming the beginner.

Other methods of joining on new lengths of string

It is already known that (a) the Reef Knot is the simplest, (b) the Fisherman's Knot is sounder and (c) the Netting Knot or Sheet Bend can be used.

The Netting Knot used in this way *is* a Sheet Bend. The weavers use the same knot but have a different method of tying it and therefore claim it as the Weaver's Knot. It is very quickly tied. Try it and you will find the result is the same and the tying of the knot becomes very quick with only a little practice.

The Weaver's Knot

Lay the end of the old string over and across the end of the new. Hold at the intersection and loop the body or bight of the new string over the end of the new. Pass the end of the old string through the loop of the new and draw up tight (Figs. 58a, b and c).

But all these methods mean a foreign knot, that is other than a netting knot in the normal place. The following methods are equally sound but make neater netting.

Two netting knots

Finish off the last of the old string with a normal netting knot. Directly above it make another netting knot with the new string. It is even more secure if each loose end is tied with a half hitch to the sides of the mesh (Fig. 59).

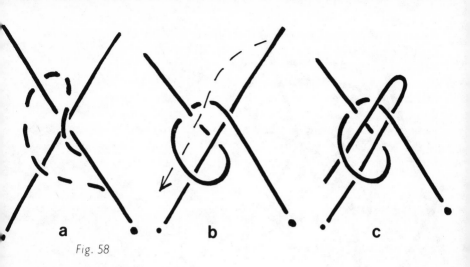

a

b

c

Fig. 58

Fig. 59

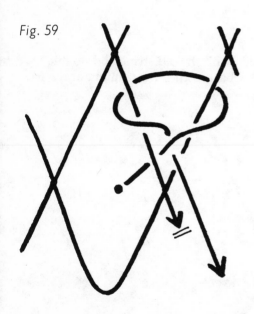

A double netting knot

(i) Take the last of the old string together with the beginning of the
new and make a netting knot with the double string (Fig. 60). If
this is found difficult, the alternative method in (ii) may be better.

85

Fig. 60

(ii) Slacken off the last knot made with the old string and double up the knot by following the knot back with the beginning of the new. Pull up both tight.

Fig. 61

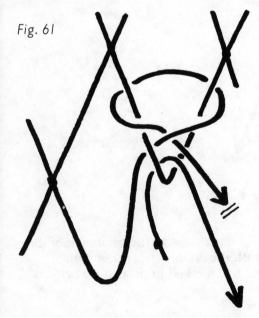

A stopped end

This method is probably the neatest of all, but not necessarily the soundest, especially with a resilient twine.

Tie a simple overhand knot at the beginning of the new string and lay it in position at the bottom of the next mesh. Finish off the old string with a netting knot over the beginning of the new string and pull up tight. Draw up the new string with its knotted end hard up against the back of the netting knot (Fig. 61).

Increasing

The fishermen and traditional netters refer to this as 'creasing'.

You are already able to make increases, but there is an alternative method perhaps not as good but certainly useful when as often happens you have failed to make an increase in the previous row. Instead of undoing the work all the way back to the point of omission, a correction can be made in the row below it. Directly below the mesh which should have been worked twice, take the working string right up to that point and mesh into it; before continuing, make an overhand knot halfway down the last string and then continue with the normal round (Fig. 62).

Fig. 62

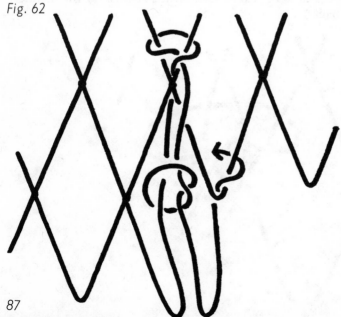

It will have been appreciated that in the shaped bags, the increases were made at points determined by quartering the number of meshes. For a sharper or slower development in shape, the number of increases can be augmented or reduced in the row. In any case a better shape is produced if the increases are evenly distributed in the round.

It will be equally clear that the rate of shaping will be accelerated or retarded by omitting or increasing the number of plain rounds between rows of increases.

Increases can be made anywhere in a row, but you will find it better to stagger the pattern of increases so that you do not have to make an increase on the drop knot. This was avoided in the shaped bags by staggering the increases with mesh one and increase at the beginning of the round, continuing the pattern of mesh three (or more) until at the end of the round you were left with mesh one (or more according to the pattern) and the drop knot clear.

Decreasing

Again the fishermen and traditional net-braiders have their own term and refer to this as 'bating'. This is done by meshing two meshes together (Fig. 63). (Compare the side strings for the handles in the shaped bags.)

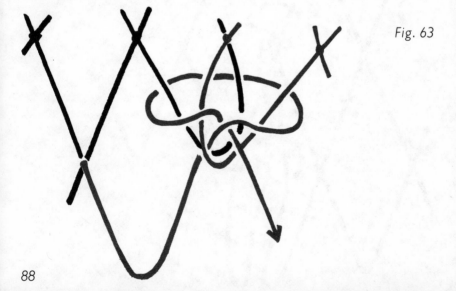

Fig. 63

A re-inforced and straight selvedge

In a piece of flat netting in diamond mesh (e.g. the scarf) the outer meshes at the edges hang loose. This is the normal selvedge, but it can be strengthened and straightened by taking in the descending strand of the loose mesh with the first knot of each row. In fact it is doing deliberately what the beginner had to learn to avoid (Fig. 64).

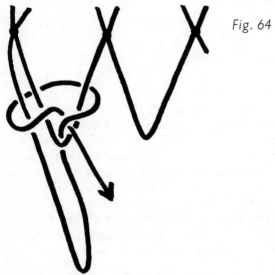

Fig. 64

Handles made separately in cane or rope

(a) Ready-made cane handles can be bought or you can make them yourself by intertwining fairly thick basketry cane. The cane should be softened by soaking in water so that it becomes flexible and will not snap. To ensure even and equal shape, it is advisable to use a former, a circle of pegs in a board or a round tin of suitable size.

(b) Suitable rope can be unstranded and made up into grommets. Unlay a piece of rope at least 10 times as long as the diameter of the grommet required. Take one strand only and relay it on itself, following the lay in the kinks (Fig. 65a and b).

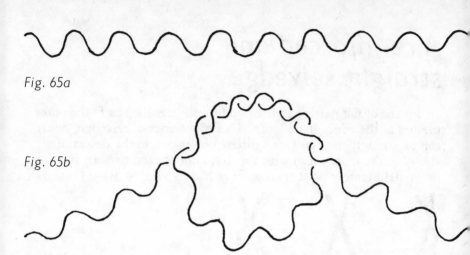

Fig. 65a

Fig. 65b

(c) Suitable lengths of rope can be made into loops by overlapping the two ends and either tying at both ends of the overlap with fine string or whipping a fine twine over the full length of the overlap.

A superior method would be to splice the two ends in a proper short splice (Fig. 66). Unlay about 3 inches of each end of the rope and marry the two ends by placing the strands of one in the spaces between the strands of the other. Tie down one set of strands while working with the other set. Begin with any one of the free strands and take it over one strand of the rope and tuck it under the next strand against the lay, that is at right angles to the twist in the rope.

Fig. 66

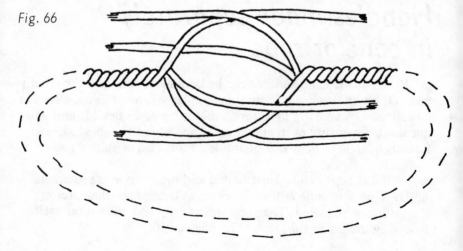

Use a marline spike (a bradawl or a pointed piece of doweling) to lift the strand to make an opening. Tuck the other strands of the set in the same way, over one and under the next. Then tuck each strand twice more, over one and under one against the lay. (Compare the single process in eye splicing, Figs. 83a, b, c and d on page 117.)

Release the other set of strands and tuck these in the same way at the other side of the splice.

No two strands should enter the same space between strands, although you will find a strand entering where another emerges.

Remember it will neaten the work if you make the casting on loops over the joint, whether it is overlapped or properly spliced.

Netting without a hook

Instead of a hook on the wall, etc. make a stirrup by making a loop of a suitable length of string and slipping it over your foot. Attach your netting or the toggle to the other end of the stirrup. When the work becomes so long that it is too close to you for working comfortably, put both feet in the stirrup and press them apart to shorten the stirrup and so take the work further from you. The stirrup is not recommended as a general practice, for you are better with the work higher rather than lower, but it is a useful makeshift and makes netting possible in comfortable places like the fireside and out of doors.

Is the mesh stick necessary?

For speed and convenience, fishermen do not use a mesh stick. With practice, you can dispense with one; convenience demanded it when casting on the bag with cane handles. It will help in the early stages to use a mesh stick to establish the size of the first mesh in the row and then continue using the fingers and no mesh stick. To hold the work, use the left hand palm down, hook the little finger and the two middle fingers in the last worked meshes, leaving the index finger and thumb for holding the knot being formed.

Netting from right to left

In some cases, it is an advantage to work 'the wrong way'. To do this, bring the working string *under* the mesh stick and into the next mesh *from the top*, DROP a loop on the left of the mesh, take the needle *above* the mesh and to the right, *under* the mesh and to the left, out through the loop dropped for that purpose (Fig. 67).

Fig. 67

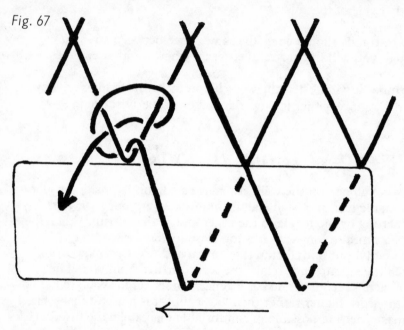

If no mesh stick is being used, the left hand will be turned palm towards you, the little finger and the two middle fingers holding the last worked meshes from the back, leaving the index finger and thumb free to help in forming the next knot.

Side strings and thickened handles

When making string handles which are to be thickened like those on the shaped bags, a neater finish can be achieved by attaching the first side string and leaving a long tail; later include this tail with the other side strings under the half-hitching, Bosun's Plait, etc. This saves a raw knot with its loose end.

Similarly, when finishing, the last side string should be tied and cut off with a long tail which can be threaded back under the thickening. A tapestry needle, or a blunted darning needle, will help, but if you are going to do this often make a draw tool of strong but fine wire mounted in a small wooden handle (Fig. 68).

Fig. 68

Splicing in new string in thickened handles

It is most annoying to run short of string when thickening handles, but this can be remedied by overlaying the ends of the old and new strings with each other. For instance, in half-hitching, lay the first inch of the new string along the side strings and continue half hitching until only about one inch of the old string remains; lay the last of the old string along the side strings and change to half-hitching with the new string to overlay the last of the old.

The same method can be used to splice in new string on one or both sides of Bosun's Plait.

The drop knot

With a tail

Up to now we have used a double overhand knot made with the tail and the working string to drop down to the next level in circular netting. This knot is a reasonable makeshift for the beginner, but there is a more sophisticated knot which with practice proves quicker and more effective (Fig. 69a, b and c). With the working string make a half hitch round the tail at the appropriate point. Maintain reasonable tension on both, but pull harder on the working string and the half hitch will re-form itself *in* the tail but *on* the working string. Hold at the half hitch and complete the knot by throwing a loop to the left and continuing as for a normal netting knot.

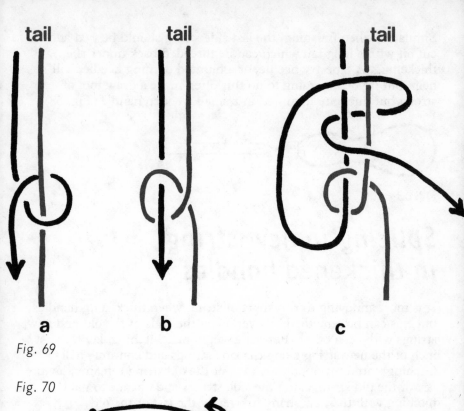

tail **tail** **tail**

a **b** **c**

Fig. 69

Fig. 70

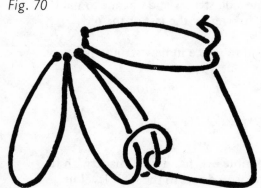

Without a tail

It is also possible to work without a tail by climbing down the last
mesh of each round and making a half hitch at the bottom of that
mesh. It is not as sound as the tail method and makes a
pronounced seam in the net (Fig. 70).

94

The tail underestimated

If you find that you have not allowed enough tail you can simply tie on another piece, but it is neater to introduce working string at the drop knot. Cut off the working string at a more satisfactory length for a tail, carry on meshing with the old tail and when it runs out fasten on a new working string by any of the recommended methods.

Difficulty with the first round after a grommet start

Obviously you will be using a needle narrower than the mesh stick, but if this is not possible or is still difficult with a narrow needle, make the grommet over an extra large mesh stick and change to the required size for the first round. This will give you ample room.

Plastic or brass rings as ready-made grommets

Small brass or plastic rings, like curtain rings, can be used as grommets to start a bag. Cast on with Clove Hitches or Lark's Head Knots. Obviously rings which rust should be avoided.

Estimating

In making up your own patterns it is useful to be able to make a rough estimate of size and number of meshes with a particular size of mesh stick. From the scale drawing (Fig. 71) you will see that the table of approximations is available. They will obviously be approximations only, because the thickness of the string used and consequently the size of knots will affect the overall measurement. However they are useful as general guides.

Fig. 71

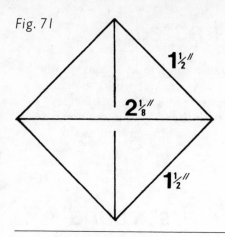

Size of mesh stick in inches	Diagonal measurement (in inches) when the mesh is square
$\frac{1}{2}$	$\frac{11}{16}$
$\frac{3}{4}$	$1\frac{1}{16}$
1	$1\frac{7}{16}$
$1\frac{1}{4}$	$1\frac{3}{4}$
$1\frac{1}{2}$	$2\frac{1}{8}$
$1\frac{3}{4}$	$2\frac{1}{2}$
2	$2\frac{13}{16}$
$2\frac{1}{4}$	$3\frac{3}{16}$
$2\frac{1}{2}$	$3\frac{9}{16}$
$2\frac{3}{4}$	$3\frac{7}{8}$
3	$4\frac{1}{4}$
$3\frac{1}{2}$	5
4	$5\frac{11}{16}$
$4\frac{1}{2}$	$6\frac{3}{8}$
5	$7\frac{1}{16}$

For the benefit of those who are using the metric system the following conversions have been worked out.

Inches	Millimetres
$\frac{1}{16}$	1·588
$\frac{1}{8}$	3·175
$\frac{1}{4}$	6·350
$\frac{1}{2}$	12·700
$\frac{3}{4}$	19·050
1	25·4

Alternative patterns

As examples of variations of patterns you may like to try the following.

Football or basketball carriers

Both these patterns make a more generous carrier.

(i) Make a grommet with 15 loops, plus the drop knot, over a 2-inch mesh stick.

Mesh 8 rows, finishing with a 9th row in double string, over the 2-inch mesh stick.

(ii) Make a grommet with 17 loops, plus the drop knot, over a $1\frac{1}{2}$-inch mesh stick.

Finish with a 13th row in double string over a 2-inch mesh stick.

A quick shopping bag

This makes a simple shopping bag of good size without increases.

Make a grommet with 19 loops, plus the drop knot, over a $1\frac{1}{2}$-inch mesh stick.

Mesh 7 plain rows over the same mesh stick and an 8th row in double string over the 2-inch mesh stick.

Quarter the meshes 5 and 5, 5 and 5 for the handles.

A shopping bag with an extra wide opening

This bag has a similar pattern of increases but the top has both sides built up separately.

Make a grommet with 15 loops, plus the drop knot, over a 1-inch mesh stick.

Mesh a plain row (16 meshes).

Mesh one and increase, mesh 4 and increase each time in the 4th mesh (20 meshes).

Mesh a plain row (20 meshes).

Mesh 1 and increase, mesh 5 and increase each time in the 5th mesh (24 meshes).

Mesh 5, 6 or 7 plain rows (24 meshes).

Divide the net into two halves of 12 meshes each and work each half separately for three rows and an extra 4th row in double string.

Halve the meshes at each side 6 and 6 for the handles.

This wider opening can be used on other bag patterns.

Other methods of making bags

From a square or rectangular base

Make a base of suitable size and mesh. Cast on with a headrope for plain netting, as in the woollen scarf, and make a square or rectangle in diamond mesh.

Attach the working string with a netting knot to the bottom of any mesh along the edge of the base, leaving a tail about $1\frac{1}{2}$ times the intended depth of the bag. Avoid starting at a corner as for the first few rounds working at the corners is not straightforward.

Work the first three rounds in the usual manner for circular netting, but with one difference; reduce the size of the meshes at each corner and for a few meshes at either side of the corners. This is best done with the fingers instead of changing the mesh stick.

Continue in ordinary circular netting for the depth of bag required, for after the first three rounds reduction of mesh size at the corners will not be necessary. With such a base the bag will need no further shaping.

Bags made from the top

It is possible to cast on the top of a bag as for the basketball goal net (see below) and work downwards. The bag can be finished by reducing to 3 or 4 meshes and tying these together or by making no decreases and lacing across the bottom.

A chain start

This is done by making one loop over any chosen size of mesh stick, hanging it on a hook and working down making successive meshes over the mesh stick in what is in effect a number of rows of only one mesh each (Fig. 72). This is turned on its side, with its two ends tied together, to make a complete round, one mesh in depth.

Fig. 72

A purist would not recommend this method as it means a band of foreign netting, lying on its side, at the top.

Bags made from a flat netting

For those who like a fish 'bass' shape for their bags or for those who prefer to work in plain netting, it is possible to make a rectangular net, in length twice the desired depth of the finished bag. This is folded over evenly and the sides laced up by tying each side mesh to its opposite partner with a short bar between knots or by knotting from a side mesh at one side to a side mesh at the other. Neither of these methods is particularly easy and should only be used by the enthusiastic netter who is willing to try the complicated in netting.

A basketball goal net (sleeve netting)

This can be made either on the ring itself or on a headrope and attached to the ring when complete.

Made on the ring

Leave a tail of $1\frac{1}{2}$ times the length of net required and cast on 22 loops over a 2-inch mesh stick using crowned clove hitches. Make the drop knot and continue in ordinary circular netting for 8–10 rows.

Made on a headrope

Stretch a thin headrope between two chairbacks or similar supports. Leave a tail of $1\frac{1}{2}$ times the length of net required and cast on 22 loops over the 2-inch mesh stick using *uncrowned* clove hitches. Tie both ends of the headrope together and hang on a toggle. Make the drop knot and carry on in ordinary circular netting.

It is not necessary to work with the meshes extended; if the meshes are kept closed up the headrope need only be small and will be more easily handled on the toggle.

When long enough the net can be laced on to the ring with the same kind of twine as the net.

Finishing off

Whichever method is used, the net can be finished off with a final round made without a mesh stick to connect the bottom of each mesh with a short bar between the knots (Fig. 73). This gives a straight edge to the bottom, but check that it is not too small to allow a ball to pass through.

Materials

Untreated string is useless if the nets are to remain outdoors in all weathers. Coated string is used for commercial nets, but a thick polypropylene, nylon or other rot-proof synthetic twine is recommended.

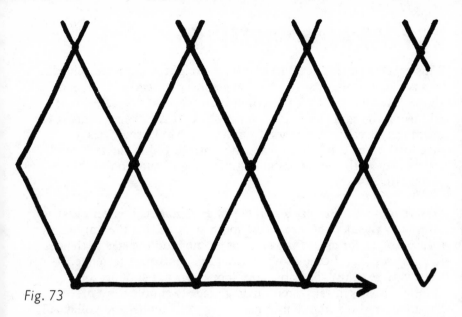

Fig. 73

Estimating

The above methods are standard for making cylindrical or sleeve netting so it will be useful to be able to estimate the size and number of meshes needed for a particular purpose. First find the circumference by multiplying the diameter by $3\frac{1}{7}$. A basketball ring has a diameter of $15\frac{1}{2}$ inches and by multiplying this by $3\frac{1}{7}$ we can expect a circumference of $48\frac{5}{7}$. Call this 49 or even 50 for simple working. From the table of approximate sizes we know a 2-inch mesh has a diagonal of $2\frac{13}{16}$ inches. Divide 50 inches by $2\frac{13}{16}$ for the number of meshes and it comes to a little under 18. Allow another 25 per cent so that the meshes are not fully stretched and this gives roughly 22 meshes.

Square mesh netting

This type of netting produces its own straight re-inforced selvedge and is made so that the meshes hang square instead of in diamond shape. This is done by a pattern of increases and decreases, but still using the same knot and a mesh stick. It is rather confusing for beginners, because it is made from a corner and progresses diagonally. For this reason it was not introduced in the beginner's course, but at this stage it should offer no difficulty to the able netter (Fig. 74).

Square mesh netting has a number of advantages; it is very easy to estimate size since the size of the mesh stick used is the unit of measurement for any of the sides of the net and the size of the net remains constant because of the straight re-inforced selvedge. It has a variety of uses; a baby's pram or cot net, a support for climbing plants, a car or tent luggage rack, a simple form of hammock and it is familiar in games nets like tennis and volleyball.

A practice piece in square mesh

Required

1 medium needle
$1\frac{1}{2}$-inch mesh stick
12 yards medium string and more according to size of net.

Casting on

Make a 3-inch loop in separate string as a foundation loop and hang it on a hook. Leaving a 3-inch tail, attach the working string to the foundation loop with a netting knot (Fig. 75). Make two loops over the mesh stick and remove the mesh stick. The foundation loop as usual remains on its hook throughout but at the end of each row, as here, the mesh stick is removed and the work turned back to front so that the next row can be worked from left to right.

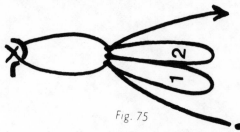

Fig. 75

Fig. 74

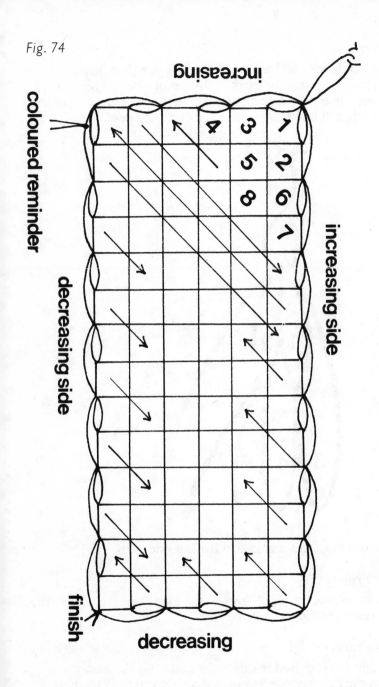

increasing

coloured reminder

increasing side

decreasing side

1 4 3
5 2
8 6
7

finish

decreasing

The 2nd row

Mesh into both loops and increase in the last one (3 meshes, Fig. 76). If you open out the work at this point you will see the first complete square mesh and at each side the double string of the selvedge which will make the side of the end meshes of the next row.

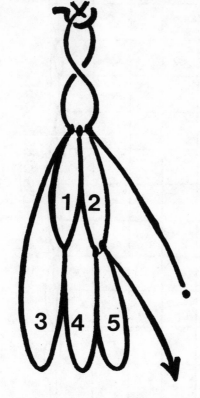

Fig. 76

The 3rd row

Mesh into each loop and increase in the last one (4 meshes).

4th and 5th rows

Repeat the same process, mesh into all the loops and increase in the last one (5 and 6 meshes respectively).

Turning the corner

Assuming that the required width is the same as 4 meshes, that is *one less* than the number of rows netted so far, you turn the first corner by meshing all except the last two meshes and *decreasing* by meshing together the last two (5 meshes).

Lengthening

The net is lengthened by increasing at the end of alternate rows and decreasing at the end of the other rows; this develops the net diagonally, the increases further increasing the long side and the decreases forming the opposite side. After turning the corner it pays to spread out the net from time to time to see how it is developing. To avoid mistakes, it helps if you mark the decreasing side with a piece of colored twine or wool. If the net is to be square and not rectangular, the marker will not be necessary because you will decrease at the end of every row. (See below, Turning the last corner and finishing off.)

Mesh the next row and increase in the last mesh (6 meshes).

In the next row, mesh all except the last two meshes and decrease by meshing the last two together (5 meshes).

Continue in this fashion, alternately increasing and decreasing at the end of the rows until the long side is *one mesh longer* than the required length of net and you are then ready to turn the last corner.

Turning the last corner and finishing off

Decrease at the end of *every* row until only two meshes remain. Finish off by tying these two together without making the normal mesh. Remove the beginning of the net from the foundation loop and with the 3-inch tail tie together the first two loops in the same manner as the last two.

A duffle-type shoulder bag

Required

1 2-inch plastic or brass ring
fishermen is excellent)
1-, 1½- and 2-inch mesh sticks
55 yards medium string and 10 yards more for the double row
2 yards thick string or cord for the draw string
3-inch × 1-inch piece of soft leather or similar material for the
runner on the draw string.

Fig. 77

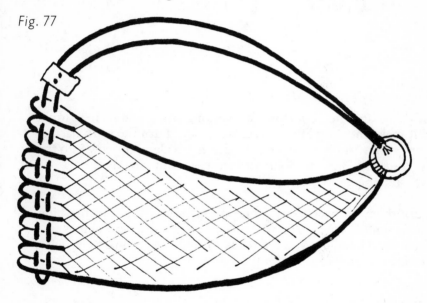

Casting on

Leave a tail of 36 inches and attach the working string to the ring
with a crowned clove hitch, but instead of leaving the tail on the
left place it along the ring so that it will be overlaid by the casting
on (Fig. 78).

With the 1½-inch mesh stick, cast on 11 loops with crowned clove
hitches and make certain that the tail is carried along under the
clove hitches. After the first mesh it may be easier to dispense with
the mesh stick and use fingers of the left hand as a gauge.

Plate 6 (opposite) Duffle type shoulder bag

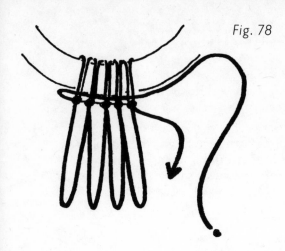

Fig. 78

Converting into circular netting

After making the 11th loop, the working string will be next to the tail; make the drop knot in the usual way. Turn the work back to front and with the 1-inch mesh stick mesh along the row into the 1st, 2nd, 3rd, 5th, 7th, 9th and 11th loops but pass by the even-numbered loops.

Turn the work back to front and complete the round by meshing the unworked loops. You will now be back at the tail, so make the usual drop knot and you are ready to continue ordinary circular netting (12 meshes).

The shaped bag in circular netting

(i)   Mesh 1 and increase, mesh 3 and increase in each 3rd mesh (16 meshes).

(ii)   Mesh 1 and increase, mesh 4 and increase in each 4th mesh (20 meshes).

(iii) Mesh 1 and increase, mesh 5 and increase in each 5th mesh (24 meshes).

(iv)   Mesh 1 and increase, mesh 6 and increase in each 6th mesh (28 meshes).

(v)   Mesh 1 and increase, mesh 7 and increase in each 7th mesh (32 meshes).

(vi)   Mesh 14 plain rows.

(vii) With the 2-inch mesh stick, mesh one round in double string.

The draw string

Thread the thick cord through the top row of double meshes and tie the ends to the ring at the base of the bag. Wrap the piece of leather round the two draw strings, between the top and bottom of the net, and fasten the leather between the draw strings so that a separate track is made for each draw string and by pushing the runner up the bag will close and can be carried over the shoulder like a duffle bag. The leather runner can be fastened with bifurcated studs or stitched.

Plate 7   The hammock in use

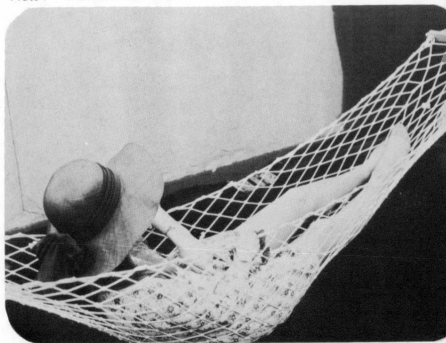

A hammock and woven clews

Whenever I admit to being able to net, people invariably ask, 'Can you make a hammock?' This is not surprising for although a hammock is simple to make, a well-made string hammock is impressive. It is possible to make a simple hammock in square mesh, but it is not to be compared with the genuine article in diamond mesh.

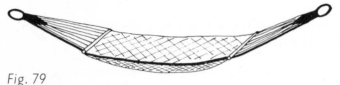

Fig. 79

Plate 8   Close-up of woven clew

A hammock is simply a rectangle of plain netting slung by means of the clews, which are the sets of lines attaching the head and foot of the netting to the ropes.

A simple form of clew can be made by using (a) a circular brass ring or (b) a rope with an eye in it. For the former, brass or other strong non-rusting metal is best and a yachtsman's thimble is ideal; for the latter, an eye can be made by tying a suitable knot, such as a bowline (see next chapter) or by splicing (see page 116).

Whichever type of eye is used, you attach to it by clove hitches 12 long loops, called the nettles, each about 20 inches long and made of thick string (Fig. 80). The netting is begun and finished off on the other set, so it is as well to make both clews first. For a more elaborate and traditional woven clew, which is well worth making, see page 114.

 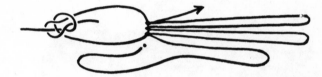

Fig. 80

The hammock

Required
6 ½-lb balls thick string
2 inch mesh stick
large needle.

1. Leaving a 6-inch tail, attach the working string to the first loop of the clew. The tail will be taken into the selvedge later. Using the 2-inch mesh stick, mesh into each loop of the clew. The work will hang conveniently by the eye of the clew.

2. Turn the work back to front, unless you have learned to work right to left, and mesh a first mesh, taking in the outside strand to make a reinforced selvedge, mesh one more and increase, complete the row increasing in each 3rd mesh.

3. Make a selvedge by taking in the tail with your first knot and mesh a plain row.

4. Reinforce the selvedge with the first mesh, mesh one more and

increase, mesh 4 and increase in the 4th mesh throughout the row.

5. Reinforce the selvedge in the first mesh and mesh a plain row.

6. Reinforce the selvedge in the first mesh, mesh one more and increase and complete the row increasing in every 4th mesh.

7. Continue making the reinforced selvedge at the beginning of each row and mesh 24 plain rows.

8. Reinforce the selvedge, decrease by meshing the next two meshes together and complete the row by decreasing with every 5th and 6th mesh meshed together.

9. Reinforce the selvedge and mesh a plain row.

10. Reinforce the selvedge, decrease by meshing the next two meshes together and complete the row by decreasing with every 4th and 5th mesh meshed together.

11. Reinforce the selvedge and mesh a plain row.

12 Reinforce the selvedge, decrease by meshing the next two meshes together and complete the row by decreasing with every 3rd and 4th mesh meshed together.

13. Still using the 2-inch mesh stick, cast off by meshing alternately into the loops of the second clew and the meshes of the last row.

Setting up for use

The edges of the hammock take most strain and should be further reinforced by fitting two side ropes. Middle a 15-foot length of thick string and secure it to an outside loop of one of the clews; lace it double along one edge of the hammock, draw it up slightly and secure it at the corresponding loop on the other clew. Do the same with another length of string at the other side. Adjust both side ropes evenly so that the hammock 'bellies' comfortably. When the hammock is hung, it needs a pair of 'stretchers' or 'spreaders' before use. A 24- to 30-inch length of broom handle or 2 × 1-inch wood will do. Cut a notch in each end and fit a stretcher at the head and foot between the selvedges.

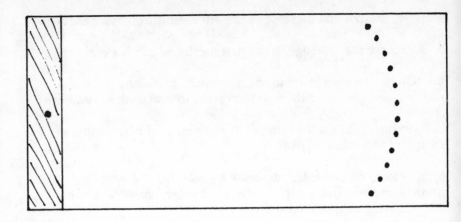

Fig. 81

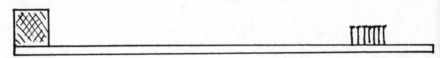

The traditional woven clew

To make this type of clew, a former is necessary (Fig. 81). This consists of a base board with a raised block in the centre of one end. The block holds a peg, nail or screw, on which to hang the eye of the clew. About 20 to 24 inches from the block fix 12 pegs, nails or screws, evenly spaced in a fairly pronounced arc.

1. Take 60 feet of the thick string and leaving a tail of 2 feet take the remainder up through the eye from below. Fasten the string temporarily on the left side of the eye.

2. Run the string round the left hand peg and back to the eye to pass up through it from below.

3. Continue round each peg in turn, taking care when you return to the eye to take the string always in the same way up from below.

4. When all the pegs have been looped, take the string through the eye for the last time and see that you have a tail the same as at the

beginning. It may help at this point to tie a temporary fastening at this end of the eye. Notice that there should be a clear tunnel between the strings where they pass round the eye. Pass the tails through this tunnel from opposite sides.

The two tails are used to weave between the single strings of the loops or nettles, in a simple cross weave of over and under, but on a steadily reducing number of strings (Fig. 82). A long ruler or lath of wood will be useful as a kind of heddle to sort the strings so that alternate ones can be raised and the others lowered.

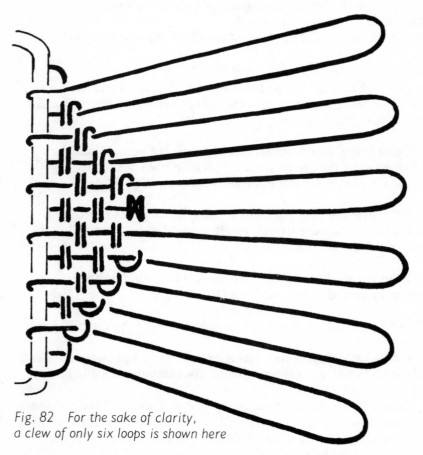

Fig. 82   For the sake of clarity,
a clew of only six loops is shown here

5. With the ruler or lath flat, weave it over and under the strings as close to the eye as possible. Turn the lath on its edge to separate into raised and lowered strings. Pass the tails through from their respective sides. Remove the temporary fastenings, pull the tails

taut and pack them firmly up into the weave towards the eye. This can be done conveniently by turning the lath flat again and using it still between the strings as a packer.

6. Remove the lath and replace it in similar fashion, but with two differences; this time ignore the outer strand at each side and use the lath to go under the strings where previously you went over and vice versa. Pass the tails through again from their respective sides and pack them firmly up into the weave.

7. Continue alternately raising and lowering the strings and omitting one strand at either side each time until only two strings are left unwoven. Tie the tails across these two and cut off short.

To make an eye splice for a hammock clew

1. Unlay the end of a rope for about 6 inches and bend the rope into a suitable sized loop with the unlayed strands across the main part of the rope (Fig. 83a).

2. Ease up the strand underneath the unlayed strand *b* and tuck *b* through under the raised strand. Pull *b* up hard against the lay, that is at right angles to the twist in the rope (Fig. 83b).

3. Take strand *a* over the strand under which *b* was tucked and tuck *a* under the next strand. It will enter the space where *b* emerges (Fig. 83c).

4. Turn the work round to the back and by easing up the remaining strand, tuck *c* under it (Fig. 83d).

5. Pull up all strands hard and at right angles to the lay of the rope.

6. Take each strand in turn again over a strand and under the next, so that no two strands enter or come out through the same place.

7. Repeat (6) so that each strand has three 'tucks'. Three tucks are an essential minimum; a fourth will do no harm, since if the strands have been cut off very close and the splice works up a little, the last tuck tends to pull out.

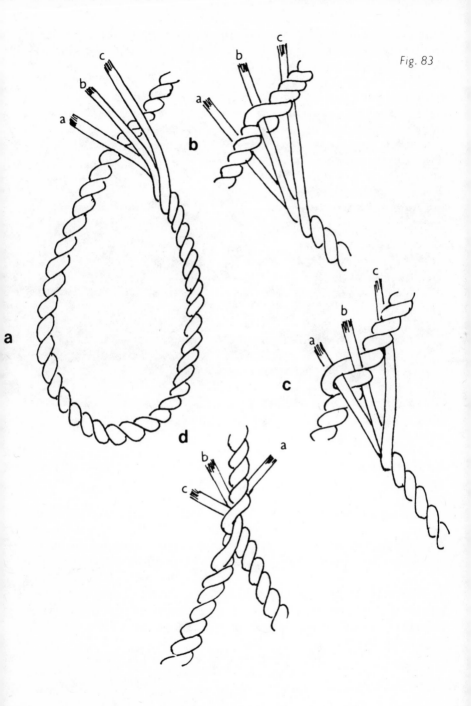

Fig. 83

Plate 9   A coast crab pot seen against a background of plain netting

The coast crab pot

This is left to the last because it is far less simple than the
hammock but for many people even more charming as a piece of
functional netting. One fisherman called the pot 'a bit of old
England'. Although the same in principle, pots are made slightly
differently by individual fishermen. The methods are esoteric, but
not closely guarded secrets. However it is a privilege or at least a
mark of favor if a fisherman shows you how he does it.

I doubt whether many readers will wish or need to make an actual
crab pot, much less a whole fleet of them, but many will be tempted
to emulate the fishermen, who honor their friends, or beguile
visitors who are glad to pay, with those charming ornamental
miniatures.

The fishermen make their pots of scrap wood bases, pliable
branches of willow, ash, chestnut, etc. for the arches and ties, and
any old iron for ballast. You can make your miniatures with
plywood bases, basketry cane for the arches and ties; you need no
ballast, but a houseproud wife will appreciate a felt cover under
the base to save the furniture from being marked when as will
inevitably happen visitors pick up the miniature pot to inspect,
admire and even request one for themselves.

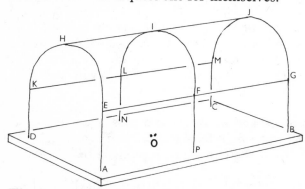

Fig. 84

The general structure

The pot consists of a rectangular base ABCD with drillings at
ADPNBC to take the three arches (Fig. 84). The arches are stayed
with three straight ties, one centrally across the top, lashed at HIJ,
and the other two about halfway down the sides and also lashed at
EFG and KLM.

Netting the pot
In an actual pot, a strong nylon, propylene or other rot-proof synthetic twine would be used. For a miniature this is not necessary and any appropriate color in a suitable fine twine will suffice.

The foundation rope
A strong line, or double twine as used for the netting, is run round the bottoms of the arches and clove hitched to each one. This forms a foundation to which all the netting is fastened. When the pot is complete, all the rope is strapped to the base so that all the netting is secured and the pot is escape-proof.

The bait holder
While the pot is open, the bait line can be fitted more easily. A couple of drillings at O will accommodate the ends of a line looped securely round the top at I; the bait is placed between the double lines and jammed down to the base with a runner tied across the two strings.

The cover
The cover is the main piece of netting and consists of a rectangle of plain netting big enough to be stretched from AD, over the top to BC and later secured along each side at AE, EFG, GB, DK, KLM and MC.

To make this, attach a working string to the foundation rope as near as possible to one end of AD. Along AD cast on 6 half meshes with clove hitches. No mesh stick is used; two fingers are a useful gauge but for a miniature make the meshes as small as you can work with.

Mesh sufficient plain rows to cover the top and ends, allowing for bracing to the sides. Keep trying it for size and when big enough cast off with clove hitches to the foundation rope along BC.

Here you will find it an advantage to be able to net from right to left (see page 92) instead of turning the pot over.

The first spout or funnel (crab entrance)
These are fitted at EFPA and LMCN to make back and front entrances. For convenience they are worked outwards and then turned inside and fixed in position.

In EFPA attach the working string with a clove hitch to EF but fairly close to F and *taking in the nearest side mesh of the cover*. Make a half mesh and attach it with a clove hitch along FP at the other side of F. Make another 2 half meshes with clove hitches along FP and a 3rd half mesh clove hitched to the foundation rope along PA at the other side of P.

Make 2 or 3 half meshes clove hitched to the foundation rope along PA. Make the 4th half mesh and clove hitch it to AE at the other side of A, *taking in the 1st side mesh of the cover*.

Make 2 more half meshes with clove hitches on AE, *taking in the nearest side meshes of the cover*. Make a 3rd half mesh clove hitched to EF at the other side of E, *taking in the nearest side mesh of the cover*.

Make 2 more half meshes clove hitched along EF and *taking in the nearest side meshes of the cover*.

By meshing straight across from the last clove hitch to the bottom of the 1st half mesh which straddles F, you begin a spiral of netting which will need no tail or drop knot. Continue netting clockwise, first into the half meshes and subsequently into full meshes until the spout shows 3 full meshes at F.

From F, continue meshing until you reach a point fixed by tracing along the upper sides of the meshes from the middle clove hitch on AE, diagonally upwards to the edge of the spout. From this point continue meshing clockwise, not with full meshes but making short bars to give the spout a firm straight edge all round the mouth. For an actual pot the mouth should comfortably admit a large crab, gauged with two large fists loosely clenched. The working string, still attached above the point calculated in the previous round, can be used as one of the lines to fix the spout. Push the spout inside and with the working string brace it across towards the other side and tie on KL. Tie a second brace at similar points so that the spout is firmly fixed at the top and hangs down to make a good mouth.

Leave the second spout until you have completed the next section, the plain wall, and you will find the cover will be fixed more satisfactorily by completing one side first.

The plain wall

FGBP is walled in with plain netting to complete one side and secure one side of the cover.

Clove hitch a working string to BG as close as possible to G and taking in the nearest side mesh of the cover. Make 3 half meshes with clove hitches along GF, taking in the side meshes of the cover. Take the working string tightly across to clove hitch it to FP about a half mesh size from F.

Mesh back along all the half meshes on FG, finishing tightly with a clove hitch on GB, taking in the appropriate side mesh of the cover. Mesh back along the full meshes, finishing tightly with a clove hitch to FP. Take the working string tightly to the foundation rope and clove hitch it there. Work along PB and in turn mesh each full mesh and brace them to the foundation rope, finishing tightly at B.

The second spout or funnel (crab entrance)

In LMCN, repeat the same process as for the first spout, bracing the mouth to FG and remembering to take in the side meshes of the cover wherever possible.

The release door

It is through this quickly released door that the baiting is done and the catch removed.

Clove hitch a working string to the foundation rope along DN *as close as possible to D*. Clove hitch 4 half meshes to the rope along DN, finishing *as close as possible to N*. Mesh 3 rows of plain netting without attaching the sides to any part of the pot. Finish with a row of half meshes clove hitched to a suitable piece of stick, slightly longer than KL so that the netting of the door can be spread to give full cover over KLND.

Before securing the door, fasten off the remaining side meshes of the cover by clove hitching them to LK.

Clove hitch a short piece of twine to a mesh above the middle of LK and tie up the door.

Securing the foundation rope

For complete security the foundation rope is strapped down to the base. In actual pots this is done by looping pieces of plastic, leather, etc. at intervals round the foundation rope and nailing them to the under side of the base. In a miniature the netting will not work up and the foundation rope need not be strapped but for realism the base can be drilled and the rope tied down with a string through the drillings.

Chapter 6
Knots

Once started on netting, the net-maker will be interested in knotting generally. The following scheme of knots was planned for teachers, but will be useful to all; it will certainly be eagerly assimilated by children. Ideally knots should not be taught divorced from their function, but knotting is a skill which children and many adults will practice for its own sake. Consequently I would have suitable lengths of string ready for them to use and examples for them to follow so that they can practice them while waiting.

The adult netter, teacher or not, may also like to have this scheme of knots to practice on, for it is true that knotting and 'playing with string' are useful manipulative exercises. It is a truism, but painfully obvious in practice, that those who take readily to netting are those who are good at manipulative crafts and hobbies. Therefore anything which helps develop manipulation helps netting and since string has such an intrinsic appeal, knotting practice is ideal for the purpose.

The Simple, Thumb or Overhand Knot

Simple is an obvious name, but why Thumb and Overhand? Presumably they come from the method of tying, and the latter would be obvious if tying it in thick rope. A more amusing explanation is the old parlor trick; fold your arms, pick up the ends of a string in either hand, unfold your arms without releasing the string and you have made an Overhand Knot (Fig. 85).

Fig. 85

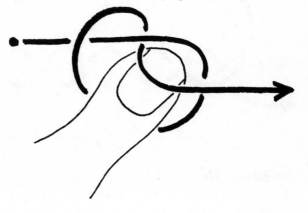

Fig. 86

The Slip Knot

This is a Simple or Overhand Knot with one end not pulled right through (Fig. 86).

The Single Chain Plait

This is a continuous chain of slip knots and can be locked at any point by pulling the working string right through the last loop.

The Blood, Bullion, Manifold or Multiple Overhand Knot

This is a recognised stopper knot. Making it appeals to children as something akin to magic. It is a useful end knot to check unravelling or to head a tassel made by deliberate unravelling (Fig. 87).

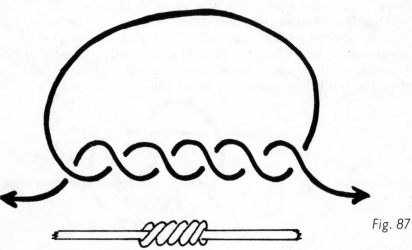

Fig. 87

The Double Overhand Knot

This is familiar as the drop knot. Note that most knots can be made double, treble, etc. It can also be made in one piece of string as an Overhand Loop (Fig. 88).

Fig. 88

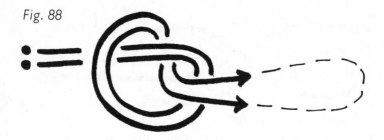

The Fisherman's Knot

This is already known as a strong joining knot, made by forming overhand knots with each free end over the main parts.

The Reef or Flat Knot (also called the Knot of Hercules)

This is the knot everyone knows together with its twisted partner, the 'Granny'. The Reef Knot is only two overhand knots made in opposite directions, that is the same working end is used first from one direction and then again from the other. The old mnemonic still helps avoid the 'Granny'; right over left and under, left over right and under. The first *right* and the second *left* are in fact the same end which has changed sides (Fig. 89).

Fig. 89

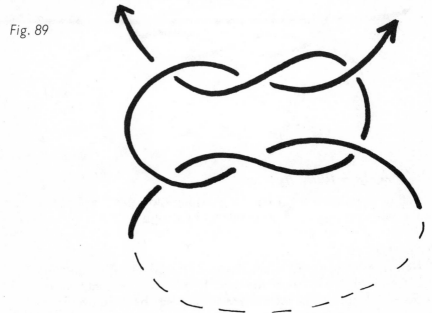

Fig. 90

The Figure of Eight Knot

This again is basically an overhand knot, but with an extra turn
about the main part before tucking through the loop. Its name is
obvious but it is a useful stopper knot, having more bulk than the
simple overhand knot, and it will be found providing a good
purchase on climbing ropes and on the lifelines on the sides of
lifeboats (Fig. 90).

The Single Bow

A shoe-lace knot. It is really a slip reef knot for it is only a reef
knot with one end not pulled right through (Fig. 91).

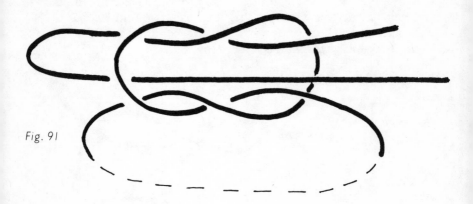

Fig. 91

The Double or Butterfly Bow

Another shoe-lace knot. Like the previous knot, this is a slip reef
knot, but with neither end pulled right through (Fig. 92).

The Crowned Bows

To the double bow add an overhand knot formed with the two
loops and it helps to 'lock' the bow. Useful with new shoe-laces.
The single bow can be locked in a similar way by forming an
overhand knot with the loop and the two ends.

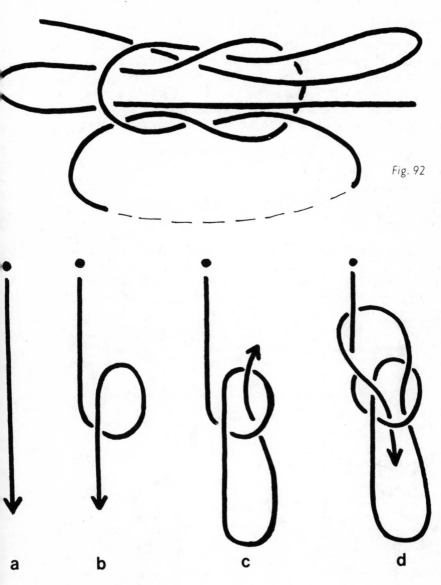

Fig. 92

a b c d

Fig. 93

The Bowline

This is probably the most respected of all knots. If you can tie a bowline you will be acclaimed as one who knows his knots. It is in fact an elaborate form of overhand knot for the working string is taken in and out through a loop in the main part during the making of an overhand knot. Most people find the knot difficult at first and it is not only children who use the story mnemonic:

there was a tree
with a hole in *front* of it.
A rabbit popped out of the hole,
ran round behind the tree and popped back into the hole
(Fig. 93a, b, c, d).

A bowline can be tied in a more sophisticated fashion by laying the working end over the main part, nipping the intersection with finger and thumb and rotating the main part into a loop over the working end. Finish off in the ordinary way (Fig. 94).

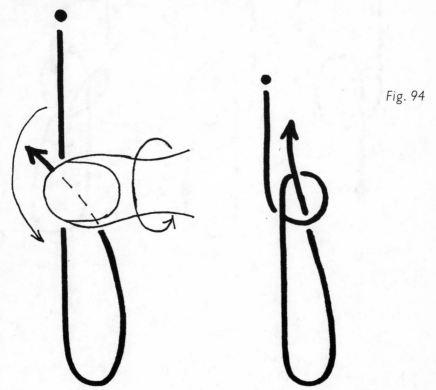

Fig. 94

The Half Hitch

This is an uncompleted overhand knot, made over a line or stick etc., and can be made over or under (Fig. 95).

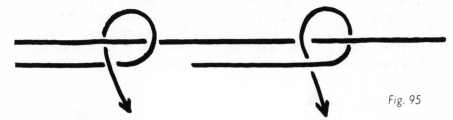

Fig. 95

The Clove Hitch

This is a couple of half hitches *of the same kind*, i.e. both made over or both made under (Fig. 96). (If one half hitch is reversed it forms a Lark's Head Knot—see below.)

Fig. 96

Children enjoy making a clove hitch by 'lassoing' a finger by throwing a loop over the index finger and following it with a second loop (Fig. 97).

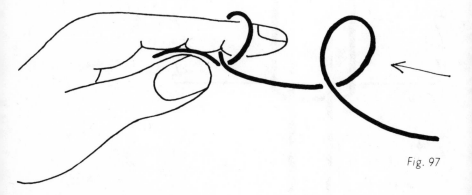

Fig. 97

The Constrictor Knot

This is a clove hitch with an overhand knot under the bar or crossing strand (Fig. 98a and b). First make a clove hitch, then with the two free ends make an overhand knot. It is useful for securing or seizing and therefore widely used in decorative knotting; for instance we could use it to fasten the middle of a string for Bosun's Plait. It is used for fastening the neck of a bag and in such cases can be pre-formed and slipped into place and pulled taut.

Fig. 98

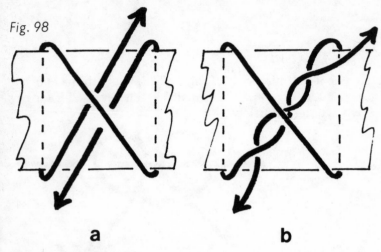

a   **b**

The Lark's Head Knot

A more attractive name than its alternative Cow Hitch (Fig. 99).

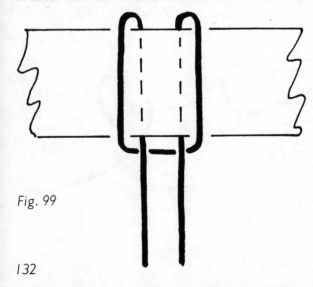

Fig. 99

132

Contrast this knot with the clove hitch and see it also as a broken or 'spilled' reef knot. It is useful for a quick hitch in a loop, for instance putting a string loop on cane handles to hang on a hook and for casting on loops on a ready made grommet (Fig. 100).

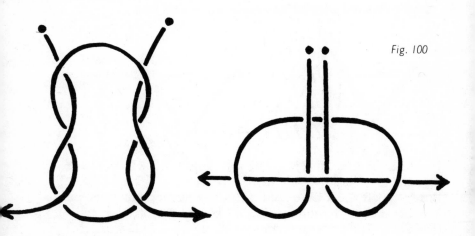

Fig. 100

The Sheet Bend

This is already familiar in form as a netting knot, but it helps to see it also as a modified reef knot (Fig. 101).

Fig. 101

The Turk's Head

This is probably the best known of all the decorative knots. Supposedly named after the turban headdress, it looks extremely complicated but once mastered it is easy to make and its fascination so great that you have to resist the temptation to put a Turk's Head everywhere (Fig. 102).

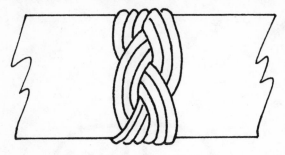

Fig. 102

Incidentally decorative knotting is a subject in itself. We have dipped into it and used alternate half hitching, or 'coxcombing', Bosun's Plait and I have known handles on shopping bags finished at either end with miniature Turk's Heads to neaten the ends of the thickening. It may be another string activity to follow on from netting.

1. Start with a clove hitch and break it by withdrawing the end *a* from under the bar or crossing, passing it over the bar and tucking it under *b* (Fig. 103a and b).

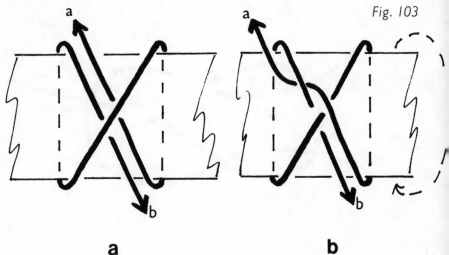

Fig. 103

a **b**

2. Turn to the back of the work and pass the right strand over the left or in other words towards *a* (Fig. 103c and d).

Fig. 103

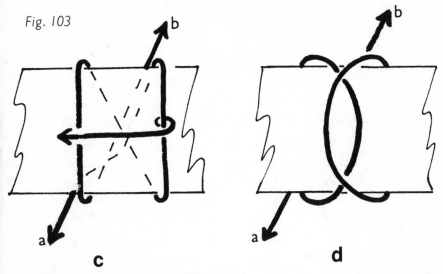

c

d

3. Pass *a* over and under (Fig. 103e).

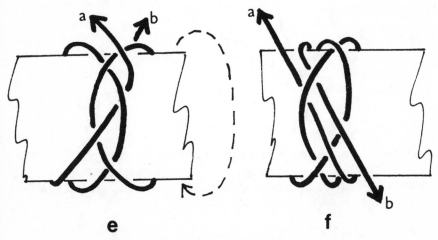

e

f

4. Turn to the front of the work again and once more pass *a* over and under so that *a* and *b* lie side by side, each ready to run back along each other's track (Fig. 103f). This is in fact what they do. First work *a* back along *b*, following the same over and under pattern as *b* and being careful to lay *a* always on the same side of *b* until you return to the starting point. Now take *b* along *a* in the other direction, taking the same care with the over and under and

positioning of *b*. On returning to the start, the knot will have been trebled and needs only to be worked up tight and the ends can be cut off short enough to be unseen.

A simple conker project

If conkers are in season, you need only a supply of *thick* string and a gimlet and knots have a real purpose.

Thick string is important to reduce cutting when playing and conkers need to be bored, not punched as they are usually with a nail, to avoid starting dangerous splits.

A good seat is important below the conker to stop pulling through so a bulky knot is needed. An overhand knot is inadequate and children try, mostly unsuccessfully, to pile one overhand knot on another. They jump at the suggestion of a figure of eight knot or a blood (bullion or manifold) knot.

Fig. 104

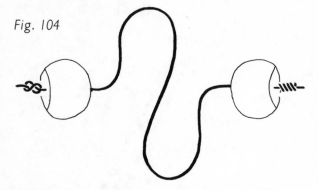

A good grip is important and they will welcome a chain plait handle, a bowline or a double overhand loop for a finger loop, or even a double-ender where one conker is in play with a second as a handle, which is also a reserve if needed.